FACTS AT YOUR FINGERTIPS

COLD WAR

FACTS AT YOUR FINGERTIPS

COLD WAR

BROWN
BEAR
BOOKS

Published by Brown Bear Books

An imprint of

The Brown Reference Group Ltd

68 Topstone Road

Redding

Connecticut

06896

USA

www.brownreference.com

© 2009 The Brown Reference Group Ltd

Library of Congress Cataloging-in-Publication Data available upon request.

ISBN-13 978-1-933834-52-8

Author: Steve Crawford
Editorial Director: Lindsey Lowe
Senior Managing Editor: Tim Cooke
Designer: Sarah Williams
Editor: Dennis Cove

Printed in the United States of America

CONTENTS

The antagonistic relationship that existed between the United States and the Soviet Union after World War II (1939–1945) was called the Cold War. The war was dubbed "cold" because the two sides never actually came into direct armed conflict. The Cold War may be said to have lasted until the fall of the Berlin Wall in 1989 and the rapid crumbling of the Soviet Union in the two years that followed, but it was at its most intense in the 1950s and 1960s.

Postwar situation

World War II ended in victory for the Allies over the Axis powers, but the victors were in fact a highly unstable coalition between the democracies of the West and the communist empire ruled from Moscow. In the immediate postwar era, two superpowers faced each other across a much altered political landscape. The actions of the Soviet Union in the aftermath of the war appeared to pose a direct challenge to the interests of the United States. The defeat of Adolf Hitler's regime in Nazi Germany had left a vacuum in Eastern Europe that had been filled, in the closing stages of the war, by the Soviet Red Army. The Soviet Union, after its tremendous losses in the war, wished to secure the lands on its western borders as a buffer zone against future invasion. By 1948, after a communist coup in Czechoslovakia, all of Eastern Europe from the Baltic states of Estonia, Latvia, and Lithuania in the north to Romania and Yugoslavia in the south had been brought under effective Soviet rule. Germany itself was divided, half in the western camp, half in the eastern.

However, in the eyes of most American politicians the threat posed by the Soviet Union was not simply a territorial one. Underlying the rivalry between the two powers was the ideological divide between democratic, capitalist America and the totalitarian, communist Soviet empire that led both sides to conclude that they were involved in a struggle for global political supremacy.

Overlying this ideological battle was a new peril—the threat posed by "The Bomb." The United States had dropped two atomic bombs on Japan in August 1945. The Soviet Union successfully tested its own A-bomb in August 1949. Thereafter the world faced the genuine possibility of self-destruction if the two Superpowers ever clashed militarily. That threat gave the Cold War a terrifying extra dimension, and ensured that the rivalry between the two powers was unlike any other in history.

Start of the Cold War

It is difficult to give an exact date for the start of the Cold War. As early as August 1945, the Soviet official Mikhail Kalinin told a meeting of the Moscow Communist Party that "the perils of capitalist encirclement" of the world's only socialist state had not disappeared with the defeat of Germany and the end of World War II. A few months later Soviet foreign minister Vyacheslav Molotov (1890–1986) warned his colleagues that the "roots of fascism and imperialist aggression" had not been pulled out.

On the American side the starting-point is often taken to be the announcement of the Truman Doctrine—an elaboration of the policy of the "containment" of communism first articulated by George Kennan in 1946. In a message to Congress on March 12, 1947, President Harry S. Truman declared that the United States was ready to replace a weakened United Kingdom as the international defender of the independence of Greece and Turkey against communist insurgency. Truman then stated that he intended to bring within the military

Marxist President Allende of Chile (center) outside the La Moneda presidential palace during the CIA-organized coup that brought a right-wing military government to power in the country.

embrace of the United States all "free peoples who are resisting attempted subjugation by armed minorities or by outside pressures."

The United States led the formation of the North Atlantic Treaty Organization in 1949. NATO was a joint military group. Its purpose was to defend against Soviet forces in Europe. The first members of NATO were Belgium, Britain, Canada, Denmark, France, Iceland, Italy, Luxembourg, the Netherlands, Portugal, and the United States. The Soviet Union and its east European allies formed their own joint military group—the Warsaw Pact—six years later.

A global battleground

Both sides actively tried to influence political and economic developments around the world. Thus the Soviet Union provided military, economic, and technical aid to communist governments in Asia. The United States then helped eight Asian nations fight communism by establishing the Southeast Asia Treaty Organization. In the middle 1950s, the United States began sending military advisers to help South Vietnam defend itself against communist North Vietnam. That aid would later expand into a long period of U.S. involvement in Vietnam.

The Cold War also affected the Middle East. In the 1950s, both East and West offered aid to Egypt to build the Aswan High Dam on the River Nile. The West canceled its offer, however, after Egypt bought weapons from the communist government of Czechoslovakia. Egyptian president Gamal Abdel Nasser (1918-1970) then seized control of the company that operated the Suez Canal. A few months later, Israel invaded Egypt. France and Britain joined the invasion. For once, the United States and the Soviet Union agreed on a major issue. Both supported a United Nations resolution demanding an immediate ceasefire. The Suez Crisis was a political victory for the Soviets. Soviet support for Egypt gained new friends in the Arab world.

In the 1960s the world came close to nuclear war. President John F. Kennedy followed Eisenhower as president in 1961. During his early days in office, Cuban exiles invaded Cuba from the United States. They wanted to oust the government of Fidel Castro, set up after a revolution in 1959. The exiles had been trained by America's Central Intelligence Agency (CIA). The United States failed to send military planes to protect them during the invasion. As a result, they failed.

In Europe, meanwhile, tens of thousands of East Germans had fled to the West. East Germany's communist government decided to stop them. It built the Berlin Wall to divide the eastern and western parts of the city. Perhaps more than anything else, the Berlin Wall came to symbolize the Cold War.

During Kennedy's second year in office, U.S. intelligence reports discovered Soviet missiles in Cuba. The Soviet Union denied they were there; U.S. photographs proved they were. The Cuban Missile Crisis easily could have resulted in a nuclear war, but it ended after a week. Soviet leader Nikita Khrushchev (1874-1971) agreed to remove the missiles if the United States agreed not to interfere in Cuba.

Decades of stagnation

The 1970s and 1980s saw an easing of tensions between East and West, although both sides still supported conflicts in Asia, the Middle East, Latin America, and Africa to further their interests. These wars resulted in tens of thousands of military and civilian deaths caused by Soviet and U.S. weaponry and often wrecked local economies.

A major change in the Cold War took place in 1985, when Mikhail Gorbachev became leader of the Soviet Union. Gorbachev held four meetings with U.S. president Ronald Reagan. He withdrew Soviet forces from Afghanistan and signed agreements with the United States agreeing to reduce the nuclear arsenal. By 1989 there was widespread unrest in Eastern European countries. Gorbachev did not intervene as they cut their ties with the Soviet Union (by now the Soviet economy was effectively bankrupt). In less than a year, East and West Germany became one nation again. A few months after that, the Warsaw Pact was dissolved. The Soviet Union limped on for two more years, but in 1991 dissolved itself. The Cold War had come to an end, communism had been defeated, and a new world order came into being.

At the end of World War II in 1945, much of Europe lay in ruins. The economies of the warring nations were shattered and millions of people were homeless. The old power structure was gone forever, and the United States found itself as one of the world's two "superpowers". The other was the Soviet Union, which the Red Army's advance to Berlin in 1945 had left in control of much of Eastern Europe.

During the war, the United States and the Soviet Union had forged an alliance to defeat the Nazis, even though Soviet communism was directly opposed to the capitalism of the United States. When the war ended, tensions between the two powers soon surfaced. After the defeat of Germany in May 1945, the Allied leaders met at Potsdam, outside Berlin, in July. Harry S. Truman had become U.S. president after the death of Franklin D. Roosevelt in April. During the conference, Clement Attlee was elected to replace Winston Churchill as prime minister of Britain.

The Potsdam Conference

At Potsdam, the leaders split Germany into four zones, or sectors, governed by the United States, Britain, France, and the Soviet Union. The capital, Berlin, lay in the Soviet sector, but was also divided into four zones of Allied occupation. In effect, Germany was split into two: the Soviet Eastern sector and the Western sector. Truman left the conference suspicious that the Soviet leader, Joseph Stalin, would not keep his promise to permit democratic states in Eastern Europe. Some historians believe Truman's suspicions partly explain his decision to drop atomic bombs on Japan in August 1945. They say that not only did he want to defeat Japan, he also wanted to show Stalin that the United States had the ability to resist the expansion of Soviet influence in Europe.

By the end of 1945, the Soviet leadership decided that their nation had to be protected from capitalist imperialism by establishing communist states in Eastern Europe to act as a buffer between the Soviet

Winston Churchill makes his "Iron Curtain" speech at Westminster College, Fulton, Missouri, on March 5, 1946. Russian historians date the beginning of the Cold War from this speech.

Union and the West. In a speech in March 1946, former British prime minister Winston Churchill referred to the division of Europe by an "iron curtain." Fear of communism hardened, and U.S. financier Bernard Baruch gave a name to the tense hostility between the United States and the Soviet Union, saying: "Today we are in the midst of a cold war."

Truman was concerned about communist influence in other states, such as Greece and Turkey. He felt that the best way to limit Soviet influence was a policy of "containment." In March 1947 he laid out the Truman Doctrine, stating that the United States would support "free peoples" fighting to resist "aggressive movements that seek to impose on them totalitarian regimes." He then sent aid to Turkey and Greece to help to stop communist uprisings there.

The Soviet iron grip

In Eastern Europe, meanwhile, the Soviet Union consolidated its influence. The governments that emerged there after the war soon became dominated by communists, backed by the tanks of the Red Army. The Soviets staged a series of elections in Eastern Europe. They were not "free" and returned communist governments. By the summer of 1948, nearly all of Eastern Europe was ruled by Soviet-controlled communist parties.

The Soviet response to the Truman Doctrine was to establish the Cominform (Communist Information Bureau) in 1947 to bring Eastern Europe more tightly under Soviet influence. Cominform nations were to trade only with other member states, and contact with noncommunist countries was discouraged. Yugoslavia, however, was different. The country had been liberated from the Nazis by communist partisans, led by Josip Broz (known as Tito), rather than by the Soviet Red Army. In 1948, the Soviets accused Tito of being "unfriendly" toward the Soviet Union, and Tito quickly withdrew Yugoslavia from the Cominform.

In Berlin, meanwhile, the Soviets demonstrated their intention to drive the Western powers from the city. Early in 1948, they blocked all land routes to Berlin through East Germany. The Allies were forced to organize a huge airlift to fly supplies into the city.

POTSDAM CONFERENCE

At Potsdam tensions arose between the Soviet Union and the Western powers. The leader of the USSR, Joseph Stalin, is at the far side of the table, with moustache.

The final meeting of the Allied war leaders took place in July 1945 in Potsdam, near Berlin. Despite victory, the alliance was severely strained. The leaders met to plan the postwar world, but each was motivated largely by self interest. U.S. president Harry S. Truman and Soviet dictator Joseph Stalin met with new British prime minister, Clement Attlee. In many ways, Stalin was the winner at Potsdam, shifting the Soviet border west into Poland and strengthening his influence over eastern Europe. As to the ongoing war with Japan, Truman told Stalin about the U.S. development of the atomic bomb. At Potsdam, Stalin also agreed that Soviet forces would soon attack Japan. They did so on August 8–9.

JOSEPH STALIN

Joseph Stalin (1879-1953), the dictator of the Soviet Union, had made a significant contribution toward the defeat of Nazi Germany, predominantly by keeping his country fighting when it appeared that the Nazis would triumph on the Eastern Front. Throughout World War II, he viewed the Western Allies with suspicion, often accusing them of postponing the second front in Europe because they wanted to see the Soviet Union bled white. Always putting his own interests first, he made exorbitant demands when it came to Lend-Lease war supplies, and planned the final Soviet offensives of the war with a Russian-dominated postwar Europe in mind.

After the war, Stalin quickly moved to consolidate his position by removing famous wartime commanders from their posts, and so figures such as Zhukov, Rokossovsky, Meretskov, Vatutin, and Konev disappeared from public view. He also did not forget about those Soviet nationals who, in his view, had collaborated with the enemy. He insisted that the British and Americans adhere strictly to the terms of the Yalta Agreement, which they did, even though they knew that repatriation of Soviet citizens would mean death or imprisonment for those returned. Thus, between 1945 and 1947, 2,272,000 Soviet citizens were returned by the Western Allies to the Soviet Union. One-fifth were either shot or given 25-year sentences in the gulag. Stalin's paranoia grew as he instigated fresh repressions against peasants, intellectuals and Jews, hundreds of the latter being shot between 1951 and Stalin's death in March 1953.

CHURCHILL'S "IRON CURTAIN" SPEECH

Winston Churchill's speech in Fulton, Missouri, on March 5, 1946, introduced the world to the term "iron curtain." Churchill had already used the phrase the previous year in a letter to U.S. president Franklin D. Roosevelt. The phrase had, however, first been coined by a British socialist named Ethel Snowden in 1919.

Churchill was no longer British prime minister when he made the speech, although he still had great prestige on the world stage. By March 1946, communist coalition governments had been established in Poland, Hungary, Romania, Bulgaria, and Albania. Churchill said of this communist takeover: "From Stettin in the Baltic to Trieste in the Adriatic, an iron curtain has descended across the continent." The capitals of central Europe—Berlin, Prague, Budapest, Belgrade, Bucharest, and Sofia—were all under the influence of Moscow. Churchill acknowledged Stalin's right to strengthen his western borders, but also warned of the dangers of the spread of Soviet influence and called for a Western alliance to withstand the communist threat. Churchill's plea came only a year after the Allied conference at Potsdam at the end of World War II.

Stalin denounced the speech, calling Churchill a warmonger and accusing the Allies of breaking faith over promises made at Potsdam. They had not, for example, shared the secrets of the atomic bomb. Allied leaders claimed it was Stalin who had broken faith.

WINSTON CHURCHILL

Winston Churchill (1875-1965) was one of the greatest political figures of the 20th century. The prime minister of Britain and leader of the British Empire during World War II, Churchill made his "Iron Curtain" speech in 1946 when he was actually out of office, having been defeated in the general election of 1945 by the Labour leader, Clement Attlee. The reason that the speech was so important was that Churchill's opinions were still enormously influential, especially when it came to international affairs. Churchill recognized the evils of communism and that the West should do all it could to prevent the Soviet Union from taking over the whole of Europe. This meant confrontation, which the U.S. presidents of the 1950s, Harry S. Truman and Dwight D. Eisenhower, were unwilling to accept. There is little doubt that Churchill was also frustrated by the plight of Poland, which, by 1946, was under communist control. Britain had declared war on Germany in 1939 to defend Poland's freedom. However, Poland had been liberated by the Soviet Union and was now under Soviet influence. Britain could do nothing to assist the Polish people.

Returning to office as Conservative prime minister in 1951, Winston Churchill made great efforts to build a "special relationship" with the United States, believing that together the two countries could stop the spread of communism.

NOVIKOV TELEGRAM

On September 27, 1946, the Soviet ambassador in the U.S. capital, Washington, D.C., Nikolai Novikov, drafted a telegram to his superiors in Moscow. He tried to explain what he saw as the aims of U.S. foreign policy. Long and rambling, it included the following extract: "The foreign policy of the United States, which reflects the imperialist tendencies of American monopolistic capital, is characterized in the postwar period by a striving for world supremacy. This is the real meaning of the many statements by President Truman and other representatives of American ruling circles; that the United States has the right to lead the world. All the forces of American diplomacy—the army, the air force, the navy, industry, and science—are enlisted in the service of this foreign policy."

The telegram was intercepted by U.S. intelligence, and an article in rebuttal was published in the *Foreign Affairs* journal in July of 1947 by an anonymous author under the acronym "X," later to be unveiled as George Kennan, the U.S. diplomat in Moscow. The telegram and its rebuttal highlighted the growing tension and mistrust between the United States and the Soviet Union.

FRICTION OVER IRAN

Following the Soviet Union's entry into World War II on the Allied side after the German invasion of the USSR in June 1941, Iran became strategically important. In particular, the newly opened Trans-Iranian Railroad was an important way to transport military supplies from the Persian Gulf to the Soviet Union to aid the Red Army fighting on the Eastern Front. To secure this route, the Allies invaded Iran. Eventually, Soviet troops occupied the northern sections of the country and British troops various southern sections. In addition, 30,000 U.S. troops were then based in Iran for the purpose of facilitating the shipment of military supplies to the Soviet Union. At the Tehran Conference in November 1943, Britain, the United States, and the Soviet Union agreed to withdraw their forces from Iran within six months following the termination of hostilities between the Allied Powers and Germany.

After the war ended in 1945, the U.S. was eager for the Soviets to leave Iran, because Washington regarded it and Turkey as key shields from Soviet influence in the Middle East and South Asia. If the Soviets could break through Iran to the Persian Gulf, their forces would be within striking distance of most of the world's known oil resources and would be in a position to move into Southern Asia should they decide to do so.

Despite the U.S. position, Soviet troops stayed on in northern Iran. Truman reported the issue to the United Nations, and he also sent a strongly worded note to Moscow demanding that Soviet troops leave Iran. In March 1946, the Soviets announced that they would leave Iran by the end of May.

Nikolai Novikov, Soviet ambassador in Washington, whose telegram to his masters in Moscow regarding American foreign policy was intercepted by U.S. intelligence.

ATOMIC BOMB TESTS

The United States was the world's first nuclear superpower. As relations with the Soviets deteriorated immediately after World War II, the U.S. government was eager to continue developing its nuclear arsenal. In June 1946, the U.S. military conducted "weapons effects" tests with atomic bombs at Bikini Atoll lagoon in the Marshall Islands, in the Pacific. Rather than just study the behavior of a weapon's design, the purpose of the tests was to examine the effects of nuclear explosions on naval vessels, planes, and animals. A fleet of 71 ships were used. The "Able" test was an airburst explosion at an altitude of 520 ft (160 m). The "Baker" test was an underwater atomic explosion.

The decision to base U.S. national defense on atomic power meant that suitable weapons were needed to meet evolving requirements. Weapon designs that used fissile material efficiently were needed to

The Americans detonate an atomic bomb at Bikini Atoll during the "Baker" test in 1946. Note the naval vessels in the water.

increase the number of weapons in the stockpile. "Operation Sandstone," conducted in the spring of 1948, tested weapon designs that met these needs. Eniwetok Atoll in the Marshall Islands was selected as the test site, and three explosions took place there between April and May 1948.

"Sandstone" was successful in increasing the defensive capabilities of the United States. The tests were conducted after a huge postwar demobilization of the military and during a time of increasing tensions with the Soviet Union, so strategists saw them as a much-needed boost to the nation's arsenal.

THE CENTRAL INTELLIGENCE AGENCY

In World War II, the U.S. Office of Strategic Services (OSS) had a mandate to collect and analyze strategic information. After World War II, however, the OSS was abolished. With the start of the Cold War, President Harry S. Truman recognized the urgent need for a centralized intelligence organization. To this end, Truman signed the National Security Act establishing the Central Intelligence Agency (CIA) in 1947. The National Security Act charged the CIA with coordinating the nation's intelligence activities and correlating, evaluating, and disseminating intelligence affecting national security. The National Security Council Directive on Office of Special Projects, June 18, 1948, gave the CIA the authority to carry out covert operations "against hostile foreign states or groups, or in support of friendly foreign states or groups, but which are so planned and conducted that any U.S. Government responsibility for them is not evident to unauthorized persons." In 1949, the Central Intelligence Agency Act exempted the CIA from having to disclose its "organization, functions, officials, titles, salaries, or numbers of personnel employed."

THE TRUMAN DOCTRINE

On March 12, 1947, U.S. president Harry S. Truman asked Congress to provide aid to Greece and Turkey. Both the Greek and the Turkish governments were resisting communist attempts to take power in their countries. Addressing this issue, the U.S. president laid out what would later become known as the "Truman Doctrine." He said that the postwar world now faced a choice of two ways of life. One was marked by "by free institutions, representative government, free elections." The other was "based upon the will of a minority forcibly imposed on the majority. It relies on terror and oppression." Truman added: "I believe that it must be the policy of the United States to support free peoples who are resisting attempted subjugation by armed minorities or by outside pressures."

The implication of Truman's speech was that the United States was henceforth committed to resisting Soviet expansion and communist influence across the world. Truman made the dispute between the United States and the Soviet Union into a choice between "democracy" and "totalitarianism."

As a result of the speech, Congress released the funding that Truman had asked for, and aid was sent to the Greek and Turkish governments. With the benefit of this U.S. assistance, in 1949 the civil war in Greece ended in defeat for the communists; in addition, Turkey would long remain within the Western sphere of influence.

HARRY S. TRUMAN

On April 12, 1945, after President Franklin D. Roosevelt's unexpected death, Harry S. Truman (1884-1972) was sworn in as the 33rd president of the United States. Truman was immediately faced with a number of momentous events and decisions: an Allied conference at Potsdam, Berlin; the governing of the defeated German nation; and giving the order to drop two atomic bombs on Japan on August 6 and 9, 1945. The first year of Truman's presidency also saw the founding of the United Nations (UN) and the development of an increasingly strained and confrontational relationship with the Soviet Union. Truman's foreign policy objective was to prevent the expansion of the influence of the Soviet Union and to halt the spread of communism. Thus, the Truman Doctrine provided military aid to countries resisting communist insurgencies, and the Marshall Plan sought to revive the economies of the nations of Europe in the hope that communism would not thrive among prosperity. The North Atlantic Treaty Organization (NATO) also built a military barrier confronting the Soviet Union in Europe. The one time during his presidency when a communist nation showed aggression toward a noncommunist one--when North Korea invaded South Korea in June 1950--Truman responded by waging undeclared war.

THE RIO PACT

U.S. president Harry S. Truman, whose support for Greece and Turkey prevented both countries falling to communist tyranny. Truman also confronted communist aggression in Korea.

The Inter-American Reciprocal Assistance Treaty, or Rio Pact, was signed in Rio de Janeiro, Brazil, in 1947 by the United States and 19 Latin American countries. The treaty was seen as so important that U.S. president Harry S. Truman traveled to Rio in person. The gathered delegates signed the Rio Pact on September 2, 1947, and returned to their homelands to seek ratification. The Treaty became operative in 1948, when Costa Rica finally ratified the treaty.

The Rio Pact, which served as a model for NATO, provided for collective defense against aggression from outside the region. Clearly aimed at the Soviet Union, the Rio Pact became the cornerstone of hemispheric security during the Cold War.

SIGNATORIES TO THE RIO PACT

Eventually, 23 countries became members of the Rio Pact. They were:

Argentina	Dominican Republic	Panama
Bahamas	Ecuador	Paraguay
Bolivia	El Salvador	Peru
Brazil	Guatemala	Trinidad and Tobago
Chile	Haiti	United States
Colombia	Honduras	Uruguay
Costa Rica	Mexico	Venezuela
Cuba	Nicaragua	

THE BERLIN BLOCKADE

Postwar Germany and its capital, Berlin, were split into four zones, administered by the United States, Britain, France, and the Soviet Union. Berlin lay deep inside the Soviet zone. In 1948, the three Western allies introduced a new German currency (the Deutschemark). Stalin reacted by closing all land links between West Berlin and West Germany. The Western powers were forced to fly in food, coal, and other vital supplies. Stalin did not dare risk shooting down Allied planes, because of U.S. atomic weapons. The airlift lasted for 11 months, and included 277,000 flights. In May 1949, the Soviets admitted failure by lifting the blockade.

BERLIN AIRLIFT STATISTICS

The minimum supply tonnage in June 1948 was estimated at 4,500 tons (4,572 tonnes) daily. Because of continued operational success, this level was increased to 5,620 tons (5,710 tonnes) daily by the fall of 1948. By January 1949, the city of Berlin was able to stockpile supplies and increase the daily food ration from 1,600 calories to 1,880 calories per person. In April 1949, "Operation Vittles" staged a one-day demonstration of Allied resources. In a 24-hour period, 1,398 flights delivered over 13,000 tons (13,208 tonnes) of coal without accident or injury.

When supply flights increased despite the German winter and continued to grow as the better weather of spring arrived, the Soviets realized that the Western airlift could not be stopped. On May 12, 1949, the blockade was lifted and ground transportation flowed east to Berlin. The airlift continued, however, until West Germany was formally declared a nation (the Federal Republic of Germany) in September 1949. By the time the operation ended, 278,228 flights had delivered 2,326,406 tons (2,363,628 tonnes) of supplies. The United States conducted 189,963 of those flights, carrying 1,783,573 tons (1,812,110 tonnes) of supplies, of which 1,421,119 tons (1,443,857 tonnes) were coal.

THE MARSHALL PLAN

U.S. secretary of state George C. Marshall announced in June 1947 that it was his government's intention to aid economic recovery in Europe, because a strong European economy would encourage political stability there. In turn, that would help prevent European nations from embracing communism.

The Economic Recovery Program was popularly named for its creator, becoming known as the Marshall Plan. By September 1947, 16 nations from Western Europe had identified what aid they required. Over the next four years, they received more than $13 billion of U.S. aid. The Marshall Plan was a major factor in the reconstruction of Western Europe, helping to foster the recovery of agriculture and industry, which in many countries had been devastated by the war.

The initial Soviet response to the Marshall Plan was positive, but it soon became more negative and the the Soviets ultimately rejected the program. They pressed their Eastern European neighbors to do the same. Andrei Vyshinsky, the Soviet deputy foreign minister, told the United Nations in September 1947 that the United States was "imposing its will on independent states," adding that the plan would put European countries under the "economic and political control of the United States." Vyshinsky predicted that the plan would divide "Europe into two camps."

By provoking Soviet fears of U.S. imperialist intentions, the Truman Doctrine and the Marshall Plan did indeed lead to a further breakdown of trust and cooperation between the two superpowers.

RIVAL TRADE BLOCS

In 1948, the Western European recipients of Marshall Aid established the Organization for European Economic Cooperation (OEEC) to administer the aid from the United States. The group became one of the first Western alliances of the Cold War.

The Western Europeans also united in military alliances. In March 1948, Britain, France, and the Benelux countries (Luxembourg, Belgium, and the Netherlands) signed the Brussels Treaty. In April 1949, partly in response to the Soviet blockade of Berlin, the signatories of the Brussels Treaty joined the North Atlantic Treaty Organization (NATO). The other members were Canada, Denmark, Iceland, Italy, Norway, Portugal, and the United States. They all pledged to treat an attack on any one of them as an attack on them all.

Joseph Stalin responded by setting up the Council for Mutual Economic Assistance (Comecon) in January 1949. It coordinated socialist economic planning in Eastern Europe. In May 1955, the Soviet Union formed the Warsaw Pact, its allies' version of NATO.

COMMUNIST TAKEOVER IN CZECHOSLOVAKIA

Soon after World War II, Czechoslovakia was the only democratic state in Eastern Europe. Since elections in 1946, the country had been governed by a coalition of communists and left-wing socialists. Many people saw it as an important bridge between East and West. In July 1947, the Czechoslovak government accepted an Anglo-French invitation to attend discussions of the Marshall Plan. The Soviet Union responded immediately to what it saw as a Czech move to join the Western alliance. Under orders from Moscow, the communists

then seized power in an armed uprising in February 1948. Czechoslovakia was declared a "people's democracy." The Western powers objected, but did not intervene. Czechoslovakia remained a communist-controlled country until 1989.

COMMUNISM IN WESTERN EUROPE

Communist parties in Western Europe were established between 1918 and 1923, following the Russian Revolution of 1917. The communists were influenced by Moscow, but their roots lay in a European socialism that went back to the 19th century. Most communist parties became politically popular during the hard economic times of the 1920s and 1930s.

During World War II, communist parties gained further popularity for their role in resisting Nazi occupation. The majority of European communist parties cooperated with other political groups in the war effort and during the immediate postwar recovery period. In effect, they had become a part of the political system. There was a real possibility, for example, that communist parties would be elected in both France and Italy. In Greece, on the other hand, communists became engaged in a full-scale guerrilla war against the royalist government from 1946 to 1949, which ultimately failed.

From 1948 to 1956, Western European communists adopted a more confrontational approach. They incited strikes and mobilized peasants to seek land reform. They also organized mass demonstrations against the European Recovery Program (the Marshall Plan) and the North Atlantic Treaty Organization (NATO). The communists' tactics and opposition to programs that stimulated economic recovery greatly diminished their appeal. As the economies of Western Europe improved, so the popularity of communist parties declined.

Czech workers' militia march into Prague during the communist seizure of power in February 1948.

NATO IS FORMED

The inaugural address to Washington Treaty members in Washington on April 4, 1949, during the ceremony to mark the signing of the agreement establishing NATO.

Soviet expansion, which had started during World War II with the annexation of Estonia, Latvia, Lithuania, and areas in Finland, Poland, Rumania, northeastern Germany, and eastern Czechoslovakia, continued after 1945. The presence of the victorious Red Army in the heart of Europe compelled Albania, Bulgaria, Romania, Eastern Germany, Poland, Hungary, and Czechoslovakia to fall under Soviet domination. By a subtle process of "conquest without war," these nations were soon bound to Moscow and to each other by political, economic, and military agreements. A total of 23 such treaties were signed between 1943 and 1949.

This alarmed the West and resulted in the creation of the North Atlantic Treaty Organization (NATO). Article 5 stated that the signatories "agree that an armed attack against one or more of them in Europe or North America shall be considered an attack against them all; and ... if such an armed attack occurs, each of them ... will assist the Party or Parties so attacked by taking forthwith, individually and in concert with the other Parties, such action as it deems necessary, including the use of armed force, to restore and maintain the security of the North Atlantic area."

ORIGINAL MEMBERS OF NATO

On April 4, 1949, the North Atlantic Treaty was signed in Washington, D.C. by the foreign ministers of Belgium (Paul-Henri Spaak), Canada (Lester B. Pearson), Denmark (Gustav Rasmussen), France (Robert Schuman), Iceland (Bjarni Benediktsson), Italy (Count Carlo Sforza), Luxembourg (Joseph Bech), the Netherlands (Dr. D. U. Stikker), Norway (Halvard M. Lange), Portugal (Dr. Jose Caerio da Matta), the United Kingdom (Ernest Bevin), and the United States (Dean Acheson). It was ratified by the member countries within five months. Later, Greece and Turkey were invited to join and they formally acceded on February 18, 1952.

USSR TESTS ITS FIRST ATOMIC BOMB

The Soviet atomic weapons program dated from 1943, initiated by reports about the rapidly growing Manhattan Project in the U.S. The Soviet program remained largely an intelligence operation, but it did manage to gather much information about the progress being made on atomic weapons by the United States.

The first Soviet nuclear test in August 1949 saw the detonation of a plutonium bomb, the RDS-1. Many historians consider this moment as the start of the nuclear arms race. The Soviet test came as a shock to the West, as U.S. intelligence believed that the Soviet Union was several years from being able to detonate a nuclear device. More than two years passed before the next Soviet atomic bomb, codenamed "Joe-2," was detonated in a test on September 24, 1951.

How the Soviet atomic bomb test was announced in American newspapers in 1949.

SOVIET SPIES

The development of Soviet nuclear weapons was helped immensely by a Soviet spy ring inside the U.S. nuclear program. The chief spy was physicist Klaus Fuchs, who had been passing British and U.S. nuclear secrets to Moscow since the German invasion of the USSR in 1941, believing the Soviets had the right to know what their allies were up to. Other spies included Theodore Hall, Allan Nunn May, and Bruno Pontecorvo. They believed that the Soviet Union was a peaceful socialist state and, some argue, they were responsible for the nuclear arms race that followed in subsequent decades, taking the world to the brink of nuclear destruction.

COMMUNIST VICTORY IN CHINA

China had been divided by civil war since the 1920s. On one side was the government of the nationalist Kuomintang (KMT), led by Chiang Kai-shek. Their opponents were the Chinese Communist Party (CCP) and its military wing, the People's Liberation Army (PLA). The communists were led by Mao Zedong. The two sides had cooperated to fight the Japanese, but, at the end of World War II, the civil war began again.

At first, the KMT seemed the more likely victor. It was heavily backed by the United States and also had around 3 million troops at its disposal, whereas the PLA had only 1 million. However, Mao's forces were highly motivated. From 1947, the PLA gained control of Manchuria, in northern China, which had previously been in Japanese hands. The PLA then moved south, winning a series of important victories, and many KMT troops began to switch sides.

The PLA captured the cities of Nanking, Han-k'ou, and Shanghai in April and May 1948. The next year, 1949, it took Canton and Chungking, the temporary Nationalist capital. The KMT collapsed, having suffered 1.5 million casualties in 18 months' fighting. Chiang's government finally fled to the island of Taiwan. On October 1, 1949, Mao Zedong proclaimed the People's Republic of China, with its capital in Beijing.

The dictator of communist China, Mao Zedong, came to power in 1949 and established a communist regime that still endures.

CHINA IN THE COLD WAR

China's leverage throughout the Cold War was primarily determined by its size. With the largest population and occupying the third-largest territory in the world, China was a factor that neither superpower could ignore. In the late 1940s and early 1950s, when China entered a strategic alliance with the Soviet Union, the United States immediately felt threatened. Facing a number of offensives by communist states and also by revolutionary and other radical nationalist forces in East Asia, the U.S. government responded with the most extensive peacetime mobilization of national resources in U.S. history. In its efforts to "roll back" the Soviet/communist threat, the United States became involved in the Korean War and the Vietnam War, overextending itself in a global confrontation with the Soviet/communist camp. In the late 1960s and early 1970s, the situation was then reversed completely following China's split with the Soviet Union and its rapprochement with the United States. As a result of having to confront the West and China simultaneously, the Soviet Union overextended its strength. This state of affairs contributed significantly to the final collapse of the Soviet empire in the late 1980s and early 1990s.

The **1950s was** a decade when the United States was obsessed with the "domino theory." This political theory was used to justify U.S. interventionist policy during most of the Cold War.

Domino theory: origin and first usage

The domino analogy was first used by President Dwight D. Eisenhower in 1954: "You have a row of dominoes set up, you knock over the first one, and what will happen to the last one is the certainty that it will go over very quickly." He used the phrase in reference to Indochina (now Laos, Cambodia, and Vietnam), where he feared that if one country came under communist control, then, one by one, they all would.

Proponents of the domino theory cited the spread of communist states in Eastern Europe in the late 1940s as proof. They believed that the Soviet Union (and China) were set on spreading communism around the globe. For those on the political right in the United States, the postwar world's most successful capitalist country, the expansionary nature of Soviet communism, in particular, represented a huge threat.

Theory in action?

During the late 1940s, countries in Eastern Europe fell under the control of Soviet-influenced communism. At the same time, Mao Zedong's communists were victorious in their war against the nationalists in China. Then, in 1950, communist North Korea invaded South Korea, igniting the Korean War (1950–1953). In 1953, the Soviet Union became an even greater threat to the West when it successfully detonated its first atomic bomb. In 1954, the supporters of the domino theory identified Southeast Asia as the next danger zone.

French-Indochina War

The end of World War II marked the continuing collapse of the old world order. Once great European empires, including those of Britain and France, were shrinking as former colonies in Asia and Africa gained their independence. Many in the West feared that the

Armed Hungarian nationalists on the streets of Budapest in 1956 during the uprising against Soviet oppression.

former colonies were vulnerable to communism, and could trigger a "domino effect" around the globe.

In 1954, the United States watched with concern as the French-Indochina War climaxed when communist Viet Minh forces defeated the French in the battle for Dien Bien Phu. Eisenhower had considered intervening, but he decided against it, as he did not want the United States to become involved in another Asian conflict so soon after the ceasefire in Korea. As a result, the communist Viet Minh were victorious, so ending French colonial rule in Indochina.

U.S. intervention

Despite Eisenhower's refusal to help France, in the longer term he made a commitment to use U.S. power to combat the spread of communism. In 1957, in a principle that came to be known as the Eisenhower Doctrine, he announced that the United States would help any country threatened by communism. He had decided that, in order to prevent a long chain of "dominoes" from falling, the United States would intervene when the first domino started to wobble.

At the 1954 peace conference in Switzerland, France agreed to withdraw completely from Indochina, the independence of Cambodia and Laos was recognized, and Vietnam was divided along the 17th parallel into communist North Vietnam and noncommunist South Vietnam. Eisenhower agreed to send advisers and aid to South Vietnam and backed its government's refusal to hold elections, fearing that communist leader Ho Chi Minh would take control of the whole country. In order to qualify for U.S. aid under the Eisenhower Doctrine, a government did not have to be democratic: it simply had to be noncommunist.

Giving aid to South Vietnam was not intended to draw the United States into a war there. In his diary of 1951, Eisenhower had dismissed the idea of giving military aid to the French in their war against the Viet Minh: "I am convinced no military victory is possible in that kind of theater." Even so, critics today argue that both the specific commitments he made to South Vietnam and the general principle of the Eisenhower Doctrine ultimately led to U.S. participation in the Vietnam War (1965–1973).

THE KOREAN WAR

The Korean War of 1950–1953 was the first military clash of the Cold War and cost millions of lives. While North Korea was a communist state, South Korea had a pro-Western regime. Both North and South Korea claimed jurisdiction over the Korean Peninsula. Initial skirmishes between the two sides occurred in 1949. On June 25, 1950, massed North Korean forces rolled across the 38th Parallel, which formed the border between the two states. South Korean forces crumpled, and it looked as though nothing could stop the communist advance.

On June 27, the United Nations (UN) passed a resolution asking member states to make direct military contributions to the developing war. Although the U.S. contingent would dwarf all the other allied nations in Korea, the war quickly became an international conflict. On June 30, the U.S. Senate approved a bill that committed the United States to deploy combat troops in South Korea to stop the communists. In the first two months of their involvement, the performance of U.S. troops was little better than that of the South Koreans. The U.S. Eighth Army, in danger of being cut off, retreated across the Naktong River to take up defensive positions around Pusan on the western South Korean coastline, near Seoul. The Pusan Perimeter had to be held, otherwise the whole of South Korea would fall.

On August 31, the North Koreans made a last-ditch attempt to break the perimeter. It failed. On September 15, the Americans landed troops at Inchon, northwest of Pusan. By this time, the North Koreans were retreating

DOUGLAS MACARTHUR

The son of a senior military officer, Douglas MacArthur was born in Little Rock, Arkansas, on January 26, 1880. Having performed poorly at school, as a young adult MacArthur excelled at the U.S. Military Academy, West Point. He then entered the U.S. Army's Corps of Engineers and was sent to serve in the Philippines, becoming a first lieutenant in 1904.

When the United States entered World War I in 1917, MacArthur was sent to command the U.S. 42d Division. By the end of the war in 1918, he had received 13 decorations and risen to the rank of brigadier general in command of the 84th Infantry Brigade. However, it was World War II that made MacArthur. Having lost the Philippines to the Japanese in 1942, he famously vowed: "I shall return." Over the next four years, MacArthur relentlessly and steadily stripped the Japanese of their Pacific conquests, and it was MacArthur who formally received the final Japanese surrender in early September 1945.

MacArthur was then appointed Supreme Commander Allied Powers (SCAP) and took effective control of the occupation and reconstruction of Japan as its military governor. He remained in the country until 1950, when he faced a fresh military challenge—the Korean War. In September 1950, MacArthur showed true military brilliance by landing a large force of U.S. infantry and Marines at the port of Inchon, deep behind enemy lines. By October, he had forced the now-exhausted North Korean Army back out of the South, into the North, and right up to the Yalu River on the border with China.

However, MacArthur argued with President Harry S. Truman, whom MacArthur held in scarcely-concealed contempt. MacArthur was of the view that the war should be expanded to liberate North Korea. As a result, in October 1950, hundreds of thousands of Chinese troops crossed into Korea to confront the UN force. MacArthur publicly blamed U.S. government policy for his own misjudgment and went on to advocate the use of atomic weapons. In December 1950, he presented Truman with a list of 24 targets across China and North Korea for such an attack.

Truman relieved MacArthur of his command on April 11, 1951. MacArthur fulfilled his own observation in his final speech to Congress, when he said that "old soldiers never die; they just fade away." He became chairman of the board of the Remington Rand Corporation in 1952, but spent much of the rest of his life living fairly anonymously in New York City. He died on April 5, 1964, and was buried in Norfolk, West Virginia.

northward. Then UN forces invaded North Korea, prompting the Chinese to send 200,000 troops into Korea. Thus began the second disastrous retreat of UN forces. The collapse of UN forces in Korea in the winter of 1950–1951 was one of the most humbling episodes in U.S. military history. However, Chinese territorial gains came at a considerable cost. By late January 1951, China's forces had been decimated by U.S. firepower and Chinese supply lines were stretched to snapping point. By December 1951, U.S. and Chinese forces had become locked in a stalemate. Fighting dragged on until, on July 27, 1953, a treaty was signed agreeing a ceasefire and an exchange of prisoners.

U.S. ships, supplies, and vehicles at the port of Inchon following the American amphibious landings during the Korean War.

McCARTHY WITCHHUNTS

In 1950, Republican Senator Joseph R. McCarthy (1908–1957) attacked the U.S. State Department, accusing it of harboring communists. The atmosphere of fear of all things communist led to public hearings by the House Un-American Activities Committee (HUAC). In the next two years, McCarthy's subcommittee called more than 500 witnesses to testify about possible communist infiltration of U.S. institutions. McCarthy's targets ranged from students and academics to writers and musicians. In 1953, McCarthy began investigating the U.S. Army. The Army, however, mounted a strong counterattack. McCarthy finally met his match in Army counsel Joseph N. Welch. Gradually McCarthy, the consummate bully, became the victim. The culminating exchange came when Welch asked McCarthy: "Have you no sense of decency, sir, at long last? Have you no sense of decency?" The audience broke into applause, and the chairman adjourned the hearing. On December 2, 1954, the Senate censured McCarthy for "conduct contrary to senatorial traditions." Largely ignored thereafter, McCarthy lapsed into alcoholism, from which he died three years later.

J. EDGAR HOOVER

John Edgar Hoover was born in Washington, D.C., on January 1, 1895. During World War I, Hoover took a job as a file reviewer at the U.S. Justice Department. In 1919, Attorney General A. Mitchell Palmer put Hoover in charge of the department's General Intelligence Division. In 1920, labor unrest led to a widespread panic (the "Red Scare") that communists would overthrow the U.S. government. As part of his new job, Hoover gathered information to target and deport suspected communists.

In 1924, Hoover became director of the Bureau of Investigation, which became the Federal Bureau of Investigation (FBI) in 1935. From the onset of the Cold War in the 1940s, the FBI maintained intensive surveillance of communists and other left-wing activists in the United States. Hoover reportedly supplied Senator Joseph McCarthy with much of the information on which the senator based his accusations about government officials being communists. The association ended in 1954, when McCarthy made the mistake of using an internal FBI document as part of a public presentation. The FBI also provided information to the House Un-American Activities Committee (HUAC).

Hoover's position in the FBI was unassailable because he used FBI surveillance to collate secret dossiers—which he kept to himself—about politicians, including almost every president, that he could threaten to reveal if necessary. At the same time, however, the Mafia was able to operate with minimal interference from the FBI. Since Hoover's death, it has been claimed that this was because, from the early 1950s, he was being blackmailed by crime boss Meyer Lansky, who allegedly had evidence of Hoover's homosexuality.

Although his public reputation has since suffered badly—his persecution of political reformers such as Martin Luther King, Jr., became notorious—Hoover held onto his post until his death on May 2, 1972.

ROSENBERG SPY CASE

Ethel and Julius Rosenberg passed on secrets to the Soviet Union. They were tried and executed in the electric chair.

Julius Rosenberg was born in New York City on May 12, 1918. In his teens, he joined the Young Communist League and in 1936 met Ethel Greenglass. They married in 1939. In 1940, Julius joined the Army Signal Corps. Julius was discharged from the army in 1945 when it emerged that he had lied about being a member of the Communist Party. During World War II, the Rosenbergs had regular contact with Ethel's brother, Sergeant David Greenglass, who worked on the Manhattan Project, the U.S. atomic bomb program. The Rosenbergs passed information from Greenglass to Harry Gold, a Swiss-born American, who handed it on to Anatoly A. Yakovlev, the Soviet vice-consul in New York.

All this came to light in 1950 with the exposure of Klaus Fuchs, a scientist who had passed nuclear secrets to the Soviets. Gold, Greenglass, and the Rosenbergs were arrested. Another suspect, Morton Sobell, a friend of Julius, fled to Mexico but was soon extradited. The Rosenbergs were charged with "conspiring to commit espionage." The trial opened on March 6, 1951, with Greenglass, who had already admitted spying, as the chief witness for the prosecution. When asked if they were communists, the Rosenbergs refused to answer. They were found guilty and sentenced to death; Sobell and Gold were sent to prison for 30 years; Greenglass received 15 years. There then followed a long series of appeals, but all were denied. Pleas for clemency were rejected by President Truman in 1952 and President Eisenhower in 1953. On June 19, 1953, the Rosenbergs were executed at Sing Sing Prison, New York State.

DEATH OF STALIN

The funeral of Stalin in Moscow on March 9, 1953. Prominent among the mourners is future Soviet premier Nikita Khrushchev on the far right.

At the beginning of the 1950s, the Soviet Union's communist leader, Joseph Stalin (1879–1953), had been in power since 1922 and had gradually subverted the instruments of government—the Communist Party itself and the Politburo (the executive committee of the party, which was effectively the Soviet cabinet of ministers)—for his own ends. In so doing, he had created a cult of personality dedicated to himself as the embodiment of Soviet progress. He had systematically imprisoned or executed anyone who might challenge him—even close allies—and had silenced dissent in the Politburo through the threat of a similar fate.

NIKITA KHRUSHCHEV

When Joseph Stalin died in March 1953, Nikita Khrushchev (1894–1971) became the leader of the Soviet Communist Party, but it took him several years to consolidate his position. In February 1956, he made a speech to the 20th Party Congress denouncing Stalin. It caused a sensation in the Communist Party and in the West, although Khrushchev failed to mention his own role in the Stalinist terror.

The speech initiated a campaign of "deStalinization." Khrushchev also attempted to improve Soviet living standards and to allow greater freedom in cultural and intellectual life. In the mid-1950s, he launched his "Virgin Lands" campaign to encourage farming on previously uncultivated land in the Kazakh Republic (Kazakhstan). He also invested in the Soviet space program, resulting in the 1957 flight of Sputnik I, the first ever spacecraft to orbit the Earth.

In relations with the West, Khrushchev's time in office was marked by a series of crises, from the shooting down of an American U-2 spy-plane over the Soviet Union in 1960 and the building of the Berlin Wall in 1961 to, most significantly, the Cuban Missile Crisis of 1962, which brought the world to the brink of nuclear war. Despite this, Khrushchev also attempted to pursue a policy of coexistence with the West. This change in doctrine, together with Khrushchev's rejection of Stalinism, led to a split with communist China in 1960.

Significantly, Khrushchev was not prepared to loosen the grip of the Soviet Union on its satellite states in Eastern Europe and, in 1956, an uprising in Hungary against communist rule was brutally crushed. By 1964, Khrushchev had alienated much of the Soviet elite and he was forced to retire. Khrushchev died on September 11, 1971, in Moscow.

Stalin's sudden death on March 5, 1953, began a power struggle. Stalin's heir apparent, Georgi M. Malenkov, was appointed premier and Communist Party secretary, but he resigned the joint-post shortly afterward. Thereafter, Malenkov became part of an informal triumvirate with Vyacheslav M. Molotov and Lavrenti P. Beria. In June, however, Beria was suddenly arrested, tried in secret, and executed, possibly because he was planning a coup against the other two.

For the time being, at least, Stalin's old post of general secretary of the party remained empty. In September 1953, Nikita Khrushchev was designated as "first secretary," without formally becoming Stalin's successor. Malenkov reverted to the role of number two that he had filled under Stalin, devoting his efforts to increasing economic productivity. Soviet economic advisers also convinced the leadership that the gulag system of forced labor was not cost-effective. As a direct result, an amnesty reduced the labor-camp population. In further reforms, the NKVD (the secret police) was made more accountable to the Communist Party. There was, generally, a much more relaxed political atmosphere than that experienced under Stalin.

However, Malenkov's decision to increase the production of consumer goods began to attract some criticism, and, by the fall of 1954 the policy was being opposed by Molotov, Khrushchev, and others, who forced Malenkov to resign in 1955. The minor status of his successor, Nikolai A. Bulganin, enabled Khrushchev to take even greater control of the Soviet Union. His title remained first secretary, but his power grew.

THE KOREAN WAR ENDS

In November 1952, Dwight D. Eisenhower became U.S. president. He wanted to bring the Korean War to a swift conclusion and hinted at a possible use of atomic weapons against China and North Korea if the Chinese did not negotiate a peace agreement. On July 27, 1953, a treaty was signed by Kim Il Sung, the North Korean leader; General Mark Clark, commander of UN troops; and Peng Dehuai, head of the Chinese forces. South Korean President Syngman Rhee was not present. The armistice saw the border between North and South Korea re-established along the 38th Parallel. A Military Demarcation Line was created, with a "demilitarized zone" (DMZ) extending 1.2 miles (2 km) on either side of this line. The purpose of the demilitarized zone was to keep the North and South Korean military forces separated to reduce the risk of conflict occurring again.

THE KOREAN WAR

The Korean War ended with many observers asking whether it had been worth fighting at all. The Korean Peninsula was devastated, with over five million civilians left homeless and a million killed. The true death toll will never be known. Figures for military casualties vary greatly. However, it is generally agreed that South Korean forces lost around 415,000 men, while the communist North suffered around 500,000 fatalities. According to Western estimates, about one million Chinese soldiers also died. The U.S. death toll was around 37,000, with 100,000 or so wounded.

The conflict ended with neither side having much to show for the huge losses. The boundary between North and South Korea lay in almost exactly the same position as it had been before the war began. And, while U.S.-led forces had prevented a communist takeover of South Korea, the country's inhabitants now lived under an autocratic regime far removed from the democratic ideal envisioned by U.S. politicians.

RIOTS IN EAST GERMANY

Workers demonstrating in East Berlin are confronted by riot police. The Soviets eventually crushed the workers, killing 383 on the streets and executing a further 106.

On June 17, 1953, the German Democratic Republic (GDR) erupted in a series of workers' riots that would threaten the communist regime. The uprising quickly spread from Berlin throughout East Germany, according to top-level Soviet reports and CIA analyses. As the unrest spread, it also took on a more expansive political character. Beyond calls for labor reform, demonstrators began to demand more fundamental changes, such as free elections.

The Soviet Union crushed the rebellion with tanks. In doing so, 383 people were killed, 106 people were later executed under martial law or condemned to death, 1,838 were injured, and 5,100 arrested. For the next three decades, the Soviet Union stuck to the pattern set by its reaction to the events of 1953: responding with force—or the threat of it—to keep not only East Germany, but also the rest of the Eastern bloc, under firm control.

WALTER ULBRICHT

Walter Ulbricht (1893–1973) was a German communist politician. As First Secretary of the Socialist Unity Party from 1950 to 1971, Ulbricht played a leading role in the early development of the German Democratic Republic (East Germany). Following the death of Soviet leader Joseph Stalin in 1953, living standards in the GDR worsened. In an attempt to stave off increasing unrest among the population, Ulbricht announced new economic policies that would end price hikes and increase the availability of consumer goods. He refused, however, to lower production goals for industry and construction, which had been increased by 10 percent on May 28, 1953. This resulted in mass riots throughout the country, which were crushed by the Red Army. Thereafter, Ulbricht ruled the East German state with an iron fist, and his grip on power lasted for the next two decades. He died in 1973.

FRENCH INDOCHINA

By 1950, simmering hostilities between French colonists and nationalists in Indochina had grown into armed conflict. In 1952, 240,000 French troops were fighting against 500,000 troops of the Communist Viet Minh and the People's Army of Vietnam (PAVN). Much of the fighting was concentrated in the Tonkin region of northern Vietnam, with French forces tied down near the city of Hanoi, while the Viet Minh controlled the countryside. The war in Indochina had become one of the first major conflicts of the Cold War in which the conflicting ideologies of the superpowers were played out. As a consequence, the French received huge amounts of U.S. economic aid ($3 billion in total between 1950 and 1954) to keep Vietnam communist-free. Meanwhile, Ho Chi Minh was actively supported by communist China to the north, and the aims of the Viet Minh were also recognized by the Soviet Union.

Dien Bien Phu

By 1953, France was clearly losing. The Viet Minh were regularly conducting major operations, and the French had inadequate resources to secure Vietnamese territory. Moreover, there were troubling developments in the neighboring French territories of Laos and Cambodia. France made promises of full independence to all three countries (Vietnam, Laos, and Cambodia) in July 1953.

The French base at Dien Bien Phu is pounded by artillery shells fired by Viet Minh guns.

In 1954, in a remote Vietnamese valley called Dien Bien Phu near the Laotian border, France experienced its final catastrophic military defeat and lost more than 2,000 men. Later that year, an international conference in Switzerland produced "the Geneva Accords." The key agreement was that Vietnam would be divided at the 17th Parallel of latitude into a communist north and a pro-Western south, with reunification elections scheduled in two years' time. For Laos and Cambodia, the Geneva Accords brought full independence.

However, even as as French paratroopers were losing the battle at Dien Bien Phu, U.S. military advisers —part of the newly created Military Advisory and Assistance Group, Vietnam (MAAG, Vietnam)— began to arrive in Saigon and Hanoi to train French personnel. Little did they realize that they were the vanguard of what would become a very large U.S. commitment to the fledgling South Vietnamese state.

SUPERPOWER BACKING

After defeat at Dien Bien Phu and France's subsequent decision to withdraw from Indochina, the U.S. began training and equipping the South Vietnamese Army, or Army of the Republic of Vietnam (ARVN). President Dwight D. Eisenhower approved National Security Council Memorandum 5429/2, which called upon the U.S. to make every possible effort to defeat communist subversion and influence, and to maintain and support friendly, noncommunist governments in all of Southeast Asia with both military and economic assistance.

In North Vietnam, meanwhile, President Ho Chi Minh also sought foreign backing to unify the whole of Vietnam by force. In 1955, the People's Republic of China announced the provision of economic aid to North Vietnam's communist government in the form of 800 million yuan (U.S. $200 million) after a visit to Beijing by Ho Chi Minh and his senior advisers. And, in the same year, Soviet premier Nikita Khrushchev announced that the Soviet Union would provide Ho Chi Minh with about 400 million rubles (U.S. $100 million) in military and economic assistance.

CIA OPERATIONS IN GUATEMALA

After World War II, successive U.S. administrations believed that Latin America was threatened by Soviet-inspired revolutions. In the early 1950s, the U.S. focus was on Guatemala. In 1951, Jacobo Arbenz, a left-wing army officer, became Guatemalan president. He brought in land reforms and promoted agricultural cooperatives owned by workers. The U.S. government was concerned not only about the threat to U.S. business interests and the loans that its banks had made to Guatemala, but also about the influence that the national Communist Party had over Arbenz.

In a plan codenamed "Operation Success," the U.S. Central Intelligence Agency (CIA) helped to arm and train an army of Guatemalan exiles in Honduras led by Colonel Carlos Castillo Armas. He and his supporters crossed into Guatemala in June 1954. Arbenz resigned and Armas became president. He then reversed many of the land reforms. On July 26, 1957, Armas was shot dead in his presidential palace by one of his guards, Romeo Vásquez.

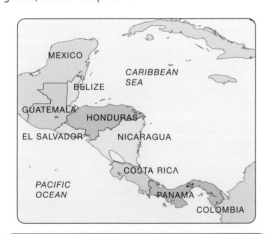

COUP D'ÉTAT IN IRAN

In the early 1950s, the Anglo-Iranian Oil Company (AIOC—later renamed British Petroleum), which was managed from London and owned by the British government and British shareholders, controlled Iran's main source of income: oil. Britain, fearful of Iran's plans to nationalize its oil industry, came up with the idea for a coup d'état in 1952, and pressed the United States to mount a joint operation to remove the Iranian prime minister. The United States was also worried about the Soviet Union interfering in Iranian affairs, or even taking over the country. The CIA and MI6, the British intelligence service, working with Iranian army officers and anticommunist civilians, toppled Prime Minister Mohammed Mossadegh from power in 1953. They had carefully chosen General Fazlollah Zahedi to succeed Mossadegh, and the U.S. covertly funneled $5 million to Zahedi's regime two days after the coup prevailed. Iran now had a pro-Western government and the West's oil interests were safe.

THE WARSAW PACT

The Warsaw Pact is the name commonly given to the treaty between Albania, Bulgaria, Czechoslovakia, Hungary, Poland, Romania, and the Soviet Union, which was signed in Poland in 1955 (East Germany joined later). It was officially called "The Treaty of Friendship, Co-operation and Mutual Assistance." In theory, the Warsaw Pact was formed in response to the creation of the the the North Atlantic Treaty Organization (NATO) by the Western Allies in 1949, as well as the re-militarization of West Germany in 1954, both of which posed a potential threat to the Eastern countries. Although the Warsaw Treaty was based on the total equality of each nation and mutual noninterference in one another's affairs, the Pact became a powerful political tool for the Soviet Union to hold sway over its allies. When Hungary tried to extricate itself from the agreement in 1956, Soviet forces moved to crush the uprising; in 1968, Soviet troops also invaded Czechoslovakia, after the Czech government began to exhibit "imperialistic" tendencies.

NATO nations outnumbered the Warsaw Pact countries in terms of total population, but the Soviet Union's readiness to sustain a massive standing army meant that Warsaw Pact forces were superior to those of NATO. However, the Warsaw Pact had little support among the peoples of Eastern Europe, whose governments had been imposed by the Soviets after World War II. Although their puppet governments joined the Warsaw Pact, the Polish, Hungarian, and Czech people in particular were opposed to it, as they were to the regimes that governed them.

THE KGB

The Soviet KGB (Komitet Gosudarstvennoi Bez opasnosti—State Security Committee) was formed by state decree in March 1954. It became the Soviet Union's premier security agency, secret police, and intelligence agency. It was not the first Soviet intelligence agency, but its job was much the same. At home, the KGB was tasked with crushing all internal dissent. The Soviet Communist Party would tolerate no dissent. The main domestic role of the secret police became to seek out any views that did not toe the party line, and ensure that those holding them were dealt with. Abroad, the KGB was responsible for recruiting and controlling a huge network of foreign spies, who were tasked with stealing state secrets from "enemy" nations. The KGB also assassinated those whom Moscow considered "enemies", including those who had defected from the USSR. In the 1950s, the KGB was a huge organization numbering 750,000.

HUNGARIAN REVOLT

Armed Hungarians ride in a truck through Budapest during the uprising. The revolt was brutally crushed by the troops and tanks of the Soviet Red Army.

On October 23, 1956, a student rally in Budapest, Hungary, in support of Polish efforts to win autonomy from the Soviet Union sparked mass demonstrations. As an uprising began, Soviet troops entered Budapest on October 24 at the request of the Hungarian Working People's Party secretary, Erno Gero, who was then replaced by Imre Nagy as prime minister on October 25. A coalition government emerged, and Soviet troops began to leave. However, on November 1, Nagy announced that Hungary was to withdraw from the Warsaw Pact. On November 3, the Soviet military responded by surrounding Budapest and occupying the National Assembly building. On November 4, another new government was announced. With Soviet support, the new regime quickly struck against participants in the revolution. Over the next five years, about 2,000 people were executed and 25,000 imprisoned. In June 1958, the Hungarian government announced that Nagy and others who had played key roles in the revolution had been secretly tried and executed.

KHRUSHCHEV'S SPEECH

On February 24, 1956, before the assembled delegates to the Communist Party's Twentieth Congress, as well as observers from foreign communist parties, Nikita Khrushchev delivered a speech denouncing the deceased Soviet leader Joseph Stalin. The speech was "secret" in the sense that it was read in a closed session and was neither published as part of the Congress proceedings nor reported in the Soviet press. However, copies were sent to regional party secretaries, who were instructed to brief rank-and-file members on its contents. Moreover, the U.S. State Department received a copy from East European sources and soon released it.

The speech sent shockwaves throughout the communist world and caused many Western communists to abandon the movement. In Hungary and Poland, newly permitted protests led to violence and governmental changes.

SPUTNIK

From the 1950s, the United States and the Soviet Union attempted to surpass each other in feats of space exploration. What became known as "the space race" began with the Soviets' successful launch of the first-ever artificial satellite, Sputnik 1, on October 4, 1957. Sputnik (the full name of which—Sputnik Zemlyi—meant "fellow traveler of Earth" in Russian) weighed 184 pounds (83 kg) and circled Earth every 90 minutes, emitting a radio signal that could easily be detected in North America. Less than a month later, on November 3, 1957, Soviet scientists sent another satellite into orbit. Weighing 1,120 pounds (508 kg), Sputnik 2 also carried a dog named Laika.

The U.S. media and politicians were horrified at these technical breakthroughs by the Soviets. The Soviet Union had already caught up with the United States in the development of the atomic bomb, having exploded their first thermonuclear device in August 1953, less than one year after the United States' own test in November 1952. Moreover, in August 1957, the Soviets had successfully tested a "super long-distance intercontinental multistage ballistic rocket," which was capable of carrying a nuclear bomb thousands of miles and delivering it to any target within the continental United States. It seemed that now, in addition to an "arms race," there was also a "space race" between the two global superpowers—and the United States appeared to be losing both.

AMERICA'S SATELLITE

After the Soviets launched Sputnik in October 1957, U.S. pride needed to be restored. In the political fallout after Sputnik, U.S. Secretary of Defense Neil H. McElroy resurrected an Army program that had been halted in 1955. Its aim was to launch a satellite. The Army Ballistic Missile Agency (ABMA) hastily modified some test missiles into a satellite launcher, and, on January 31, 1958, the ABMA's rocket Juno launched the American satellite Explorer 1 into orbit around Earth. The United States had finally joined the space race.

Over the following year, both the United States and the Soviet Union launched several further satellites. The Americans' Vanguard 1 was propelled into orbit on March 17, 1958, and U.S. satellites went on to achieve several notable scientific firsts. For example, Explorer 1 detected the Van Allen radiation belt surrounding Earth, while Vanguard 1 proved that Earth, rather than being spherical, is, in fact, shaped like a slightly squashed ball. However, the Soviets had a more powerful rocket that could launch larger satellites. Sputnik 3, launched in May 1958, weighed almost 3,000 pounds (1,360 kg), more than 50 times the total weight of all U.S. satellites. It would take until the next decade for U.S. space rockets to equal the power of those of the Soviet Union.

REVOLUTION IN CUBA

For most of the 1950s, Cuba in the Caribbean was led by the dictator Fulgencio Batista y Zaldívar. However, high unemployment and the repressive policies of the Batista regime produced a wave of popular anger. One of the first major acts against Batista occurred on July 26, 1953, when a small group of revolutionaries attacked the Moncada Army Barracks in Santiago de Cuba. The assault, which was led by former student leader Fidel Castro failed, but in December 1956 Castro established a base in the Sierra Maestra Mountains. From there, his tiny band of fighters launched more attacks on Batista's forces. It was from his mountain stronghold that Castro issued the 1957 Declaration of Sierra Maestra, which called for the rejection of foreign influence and military interference in Cuban affairs, and demanded free general elections, tolerance of democratic labor unions, and agrarian reform to give the land to the people.

In the face of this sustained revolutionary activity, Batista's clampdown on his political opponents duly increased, as did human rights abuses. By the spring of 1958, these abuses had grown so great that the United States was forced to reconsider its previous policy of support for the Batista regime. An arms embargo was soon put in place. Alarmed by both the excesses of Batista and the prospect of Castro replacing him, the U.S. government of President Dwight D. Eisenhower

attempted to intervene. In December 1958, Eisenhower sent an envoy to try to persuade Batista to resign and to leave a U.S.-approved regime in his place. Batista rejected the proposal outright.

Batista's days were numbered, however. On January 1, 1959, rebel troops led by Che Guevara marched into Havana, the Cuban capital, forcing Batista to resign the presidency and take refuge in the Dominican Republic. Six days later, having taken Santiago in eastern Cuba, Castro made a triumphant entry into Havana. On February 16, Castro officially became prime minister of Cuba.

In the months that followed Fidel Castro's ascent to power, diplomatic relations between Cuba and the United States deteriorated rapidly. Almost immediately, Castro nationalized Cuba's telecommunications network, which had previously been controlled by an affiliate of the U.S. company ITT. In May, Castro's government set a limit on private land holdings, with the Cuban state expropriating the remainder of the land on payment of a substantially reduced price. Then, in January 1960, Cuba expropriated 70,000 acres (28,500 hectares) of land owned by U.S. sugar companies.

FIDEL CASTRO

Fidel Castro was born on August 13, 1926, in Oriente Province, located in eastern Cuba. The son of an agricultural worker, Castro was educated at the University of Havana, where he studied law. It was there that he first became actively involved in left-wing politics. After leaving college, Castro planned to run for election to the Cuban House of Representatives. However, the elections of 1952 were canceled after the former president, Fulgencio Batista, returned from exile to stage a coup d'état and become dictator. In response, Castro embarked on the revolutionary path that would eventually lead to him becoming prime minister of Cuba.

Castro had great personal qualities that made him a successful leader. He was a brilliant orator and exhibited considerable personal courage and an indomitable spirit. He refused to become discouraged after his botched coup attempt of 1953 on the Moncada Army Barracks. Throughout the world, Castro then came to be seen as an embodiment of the revolutionary spirit. In the words of journalist Herbert Matthews, who interviewed Castro for *The New York Times* in 1957, the young leader personified "all the suppressed, yearning forces of his age."

Fidel Castro continued to lead Cuba for the remainder of the 20th century and was always a controversial figure. While opponents pointed to the many human rights abuses that occurred under his regime, his supporters argued that his considerable and far-reaching social reforms helped to improve the lives of his country's poor.

Fidel Castro (center) addresses a crowd in January 1959, three days after the overthrow of the Batista regime.

The early years of the 1960s saw some of the most hostile confrontations of the entire Cold War between the United States and its allies and the Soviet Union and its partners. U.S. president John F. Kennedy saw the Cold War as a global competition, and he moved assertively to reinforce the U.S. position. Kennedy asked Congress for increases in the budget for both conventional and nuclear forces, and he authorized the Central Intelligence Agency to proceed with an invasion of Cuba. After the invasion failed at the Bay of Pigs in April 1961, Kennedy approved a CIA plan for a campaign of covert operations against Fidel Castro. Kennedy also oversaw an expansion of the activities of U.S. military personnel advising the Army of the Republic of Vietnam.

The Cuban Missile Crisis

Kennedy and Soviet Communist Party General Secretary Nikita Khrushchev held an unsatisfactory meeting in Vienna in June 1961. A crisis soon followed over access to Berlin. War loomed when Kennedy told the American people: "We cannot and will not permit the communists to drive us out of Berlin. The fulfillment of our pledge to that city is essential to the morale and security of Western Germany, to the unity of Western Europe, and to the faith of the entire free world." A military showdown over the fate of Berlin was averted only after the Soviet Union surprised the Americans by approving plans by the communist government of the German Democratic Republic (East Germany) to construct a concrete and barbed-wire wall through the city, preventing people from the Eastern sector from fleeing to the West.

During the Cuban Missile Crisis of October 1962, the United States and the Soviet Union came closer to nuclear war than at any other time during the Cold War era. The tense stand-off began when the Soviet Union installed intermediate-range ballistic missiles in Cuba, in response to frantic pleas from Cuban dictator Fidel Castro to protect him and his government from the CIA's covert operations. Kennedy characterized

A Soviet tank is surrounded by crowds in Prague in August 1968, during the so-called "Czech Spring."

the installation of the missiles on Cuban soil as "a deliberately provocative and unjustified change in the status quo which cannot be accepted by this country if our courage and our commitments are ever to be trusted again, by either friend or foe." After almost two weeks of tension, the Soviets agreed to withdraw their missiles from Cuba and disaster was averted.

Yet the very real prospect of nuclear war with the Soviet Union presented by the Cuban Missile Crisis also moved the Kennedy administration toward a policy of détente with the Soviets. In the wake of the crisis, the two governments opened a telegraphic "hotline" directly connecting the Kremlin with the White House, to be used to defuse tension in any future crises. In June 1963, Kennedy encouraged Americans to "reexamine our attitude toward the Soviet Union," and in August of that year the two superpowers signed a treaty banning the testing of nuclear weapons in the atmosphere, under the oceans, or in outer space. They also promised progress on a treaty banning all nuclear testing and future agreements limiting the growth in the number of nuclear armed missiles that could be possessed by both sides.

Continual confrontation

Similar alternations between confrontation and détente persisted over the next 25 years. Changes in leadership in both the United States and the Soviet Union, and the growing U.S. involvement in Vietnam in Asia, stalled further movement toward détente from November 1963 to the end of 1968. Two years after the Cuban crisis, the Politburo of the Soviet Communist Party replaced the humiliated Khrushchev with the dual leadership of Leonid Brezhnev as general secretary of the Party and Alexei Kosygin as prime minister of the Soviet Union. The new Soviet leadership resolved never again to be intimidated by the United States, and they embarked on a military construction program aimed at gaining parity with the other superpower. The new U.S. administration of Lyndon B. Johnson became mired in Vietnam, and many U.S. officials believed that the Soviet Union was waging a proxy war against the noncommunist world, using North Vietnam as a surrogate.

In the mid-1960s, the United States and the Soviet Union had about 35,000 nuclear weapons between them, most of them far more powerful than the atomic bombs that had destroyed two Japanese cities in 1945. If the stockpile was ever detonated, it was feared that it would kill every living thing on Earth, leaving nothing behind but sterile, radioactive rubble. For many at the time, this was a recurring nightmare. All that stopped it from becoming reality was the "balance of terror" that military strategists called deterrence.

In the United States, the essential component of nuclear deterrence was known as mutual assured destruction, or "MAD." The U.S. government laid down the principle that the U.S. military should be equipped and organized in such a way that, even if the Soviets made an all-out surprise nuclear attack, sufficient U.S. nuclear forces would survive to retaliate and be in a position to kill more than a third of the Soviet people and to destroy more than half of Soviet cities and industries. Not even the prospect of completely devastating the United States could compensate the Soviets for such losses. This, the theory went, would deter the Soviets from ever attacking in the first place.

Nuclear deterrence thus became the central plank of U.S. defense policy in the 1960s. U.S. nuclear strategy had previously been based on the principle of "massive retaliation," which had aimed to prevent Soviet aggression by threatening huge reprisals for even a minor Soviet move. By the late 1950s, however, this strategy was felt to be outdated, because the Soviets had by that point built enough nuclear weapons of their own to make it unrealistic for the United States to threaten them in this way.

THE NUCLEAR ARSENAL

One danger of the nuclear arms race, as perceived by U.S. strategists, was that the Soviets might believe that U.S. forces were not capable of hitting them hard if the Soviets struck first. For this reason, the U.S. built an increasing number of nuclear weapons in the 1960s and came to rely on the so-called "nuclear triad" to give a selection of ways of delivering them to their targets. The nuclear triad was made up of land-based missiles, submarine-launched missiles, and air-launched weapons, as these were the three types of strategic nuclear weapons that could reach into the Soviet Union itself. The U.S. had fewer than 5,000 nuclear weapons in the late 1950s, rising to about 20,000 in 1962-1963, and topping 30,000 by 1967. By comparison, the Soviets probably had around 5,000 in 1967.

On May 1, 1960, an American U-2 spy plane was shot down near Sverdlovsk in the Soviet Union by a Soviet surface-to-air missile. The United States denied all knowledge of the aircraft, but was forced to accept responsibility when the Soviets produced wreckage and the captured pilot, Francis Gary Powers. The incident came at a very embarrassing moment for Eisenhower, who was scheduled to attend a summit with Khrushchev only two weeks later in Paris, France. When the leaders met, Khrushchev demanded "severe judgment on those responsible." Eisenhower took the unprecedented step for a U.S. president of saying that he personally was the guilty party. Khrushchev then walked out. After a period in a Soviet jail, Powers was released on February 10, 1962, in a prisoner exchange.

A U-2 spyplane, similar to the one shot down over the Soviet Union in 1960 by a surface-to-air missile. The U-2 was designed to fly at an altitude of around 70,000 ft (21,000 m).

SPY EXCHANGE

The prisoner exchange of Gary Powers for the convicted Soviet spy Rudolf Ivanovich Abel was an unequal deal. Whereas Powers was a mere cog in the U.S. intelligence-gathering machine, Abel was a spymaster and a master spy. He was born in England in 1903 to a Russian father who was a friend and disciple of Lenin, the driving force behind Soviet communism. In 1921, following the Bolshevik victory in the Russian Revolution, father and son returned to the Soviet Union, and the younger man was recruited by the GPU (the predecessor of the KGB). In 1947, Abel slipped into a displaced person's camp in Germany, from where he emigrated to Canada. From Canada, it was easy to enter the U.S. inconspicuously, and, under the name Emil Goldfus, Abel set up as an art photographer in Brooklyn, New York. For the next decade, Abel masterminded Soviet spying operations in the U.S., planning and directing the work of numerous agents, handling KGB finances, and maintaining clandestine radio communications with Moscow. He was such a smart operator that he would probably never have been detected, but an assistant provided to him by Moscow defected to the Americans and then unmasked him. In 1957, Abel was convicted of espionage and jailed for 30 years, but he served only five years before the Powers swap. Abel was then returned to the Soviet Union where he received decorations and lived in honorable retirement in Moscow.

THE BERLIN WALL

For most of the 1960s, the Cold War found its most dramatic symbol in the German city of Berlin. Since the defeat of Germany in 1945, Berlin had been partitioned among the four victorious wartime allies—the United States, Britain, France, and the Soviet Union. Berlin, however, lay deep inside communist East Germany, which had been under Soviet control since the end of the war. West Germany, meanwhile, was an increasingly wealthy democracy and a staunch member of the Western alliance led by the United States.

In June 1961, Soviet premier Khrushchev met President John F. Kennedy to demand that the Western powers end their military occupation of West Berlin, which would give the East German authorities a free hand in stemming the flood of refugees to the West. Kennedy responded with strong declarations of support for West Berlin. Frustrated, the Soviet leader gave his approval to a desperate remedy.

Building the wall

On Sunday August 13, 1961, Berliners awoke to a chilling sight. Along the streets that marked the border between East and West Berlin, East German workers were tearing up cobblestones and using them to create makeshift barricades. Others were erecting concrete pillars for barbed-wire fences. By nightfall, the inhabitants of East Berlin, including 60,000 who commuted daily to work in West Berlin, were fenced in. Over the next few months, houses situated along the border were forcibly evacuated and torn down. The makeshift barbed-wire fences were then replaced by a solid concrete wall—the real Berlin Wall. It ran for more than 60 miles (97 km), dividing the city and also cutting off West Berlin from surrounding East Germany. The wall was 12 feet (3.7 m) high, and behind it was a spotlit area, known as the "death area." Armed guards with dogs patrolled around the clock. Anyone making a run for it was shot without warning.

The first victim was 18-year-old Peter Fechter, who was shot attempting to scale the wall on August 17, 1962. At least 100 others died trying to flee, while up to 5,000 succeeded in escaping, some by tunnels under the wall. The dismantling of the wall in December 1989 symbolized the collapse of communism in Eastern Europe.

A section of the Berlin Wall in the 1960s. It was built to prevent East Berliners fleeing to the West German part of the city. The wall was demolished in December 1989.

COLD WAR FLASHPOINT

Despite impassioned appeals by the mayor of West Berlin, Willy Brandt, the U.S. government reacted cautiously to the erection of the Berlin Wall. Even graphic footage of desperate East Berliners being shot dead as they attempted to scale the wall provoked only routine U.S. protests. The reason for this response was that it quickly became clear that the Soviets had no intention of either moving against West Berlin or interfering with access routes to the city. In other words, the wall, divisive though it was, did not pose a security threat to the West. It would have to be tolerated, since the alternative was to risk nuclear war.

The potential danger of a confrontation caused by the Berlin Wall was highlighted just two months after it went up, when a trivial dispute over passports at the famous Berlin border crossing, Checkpoint Charlie, escalated alarmingly. For 16 hours, Soviet and U.S. tanks, bristling with weaponry, faced each other at a distance of just 100 yards (100 m). However, no one fired, and, finally, first the Soviet and then the U.S. tanks slowly backed off. One nervous or trigger-happy act on behalf of a single soldier could have had incalculable consequences. Colonel Jim Atwood of the U.S. military mission in Berlin later expressed the opinion that this incident was "the closest that the Russians and the Allies came to going to war in the entire Cold War period." This would perhaps explain President John F. Kennedy's seemingly flippant remark that "a wall is a hell of a lot better than a war."

In 1961, the U.S. Central Intelligence Agency (CIA) devised a covert operation to topple Fidel Castro, the Cuban leader, from power. The ambitious plan involved the establishment of training camps in the jungles of Guatemala, where a force of Cuban exiles who opposed Castro could be readied for an armed assault on their homeland. These U.S.-trained paramilitaries would mount an amphibious landing in order to establish a bridgehead on the Cuban coast, following which the CIA expected that the Cuban people would spontaneously rise up against Castro.

President John F. Kennedy was not opposed to the scheme, which the CIA was urgently pressing him to authorize, but he was very nervous about any U.S.

ROBERT McNAMARA

Robert Strange McNamara served as the United States Secretary of Defense under presidents John F. Kennedy and Lyndon B. Johnson in the 1960s, overseeing military strategies and policies during the Cold War and the Vietnam War. A native of San Francisco, McNamara served in World War II and rose to the rank of lieutenant colonel. After the war, he went to work with the Ford Motor Company and rapidly rose in the ranks until he was named company president in 1960. Five weeks later, he accepted Kennedy's offer to serve in his cabinet as U.S. defense secretary. McNamara restructured the military and moved from a reliance on nuclear weapons to a more flexible strategy of conventional and limited wars meant to contain the communist forces of the Soviet Union and China. The escalation of U.S. involvement in Vietnam occupied most of McNamara's time and energy throughout his tenure, and McNamara's businesslike approach and use of nonmilitary analysts rankled Pentagon officials, members of Congress, and antiwar protesters. By 1967, he was openly skeptical that the U.S. could be victorious in Vietnam and resigned to become the president of the World Bank, a post he held from 1968 to 1981.

involvement becoming known. Plausible deniability was necessary whatever the outcome, but especially in the event of failure. Kennedy finally approved the invasion, scheduled for mid-April 1961, and then, at a press conference just three days before it began, explicitly ruled out "under any conditions" intervention in Cuba by U.S. armed forces.

The invasion is a fiasco

The invasion began when six U.S. B-26 bombers, disguised in Cuban colors so as to make it look as if they were flown by Cuban defectors, took off from Nicaragua and attacked Cuban airfields. This tiny bomber force caused minimal damage and provided no air cover for the amphibious landing force, which crossed the Caribbean from the coast of Nicaragua in six ships. Despite the lack of air support, 1,400 members of the anti-Castro Cuban Brigade managed to land at the Bay of Pigs on Cuba's south coast on April 17. There they came under fierce attack by Soviet-built Cuban artillery and tanks. They issued desperate appeals for U.S. air support. This was considered by the Kennedy administration, but rejected, not least because the anticipated anti-Castro uprising—crucial to the whole enterprise—failed to materialize.

The invasion force was left to its own devices. After three days of hard fighting it was forced to surrender, having lost more than 100 killed. Meanwhile, the clumsy attempts to disguise the extent of the CIA's involvement in the plot had completely unraveled and the U.S. administration was made to look both deceitful and inept.

Kennedy accepted full responsibility for the Bay of Pigs fiasco. In particular, he blamed himself for not having questioned more closely the CIA's false assumption about Castro's political weakness, and he vowed in the future to be less susceptible to the advice of such so-called experts. Embarrassment over the episode did not, however, weaken the president's resolve to remove Castro from power. This aim was reinforced by Castro's pronouncement that, in the face of such blatant American imperialism as was shown by the Bay of Pigs invasion, he was determined to take Cuba even further down the path of socialist revolution.

CUBAN MISSILE CRISIS

A Soviet ship carrying nuclear missiles (top) on its way to Cuba is shadowed by a U.S. warship. The United States imposed a naval blockade to stop the missiles reaching the island.

On October 14, 1962, a U.S. spy plane spotted a Soviet nuclear missile site being built in Cuba. President Kennedy then announced that any missile launched from Cuba would be regarded as an attack by the Soviet Union on the United States. In such an event, Kennedy warned, the U.S. would make "a full retaliatory response against the Soviet Union." Moscow responded by saying that the weapons were purely defensive. Kennedy then ordered a blockade and U.S. naval vessels turned back Soviet ships bound for Cuba. Forces on both sides were on full alert. The question was would the Soviet leadership order the removal the missiles before the U.S. took further—possibly nuclear—action?

As the world stood on the brink of a nuclear war, several days of tense negotiation followed. Moscow finally agreed that its missiles in Cuba would be removed. Kennedy immediately welcomed the decision and announced an end to the blockade.

JOHN F. KENNEDY

Like most U.S. presidents, John F. Kennedy (1917-1963) became absorbed in foreign affairs, and after the Bay of Pigs fiasco early in his term he carried himself with assurance on the world stage. In 1963, he endeared himself to West Germans with the famous speech, made at the Berlin Wall, in which he announced, "Ich bin ein Berliner" ("I am a citizen of Berlin"). Kennedy later shared credit with Soviet leader Nikita Khrushchev for bringing the Cuban Missile Crisis of 1962 to a safe resolution, after which he signed the first nuclear test ban treaty in 1963. In so doing he began the process, known as détente, of easing Cold War tensions with the Soviet Union. He increased military aid to South Vietnam, but whether he would have kept the United States out of the Asian mire toward which he started it is an unanswerable question.

John F. Kennedy's assassination on November 22, 1963, was greeted by shock around the world. His reputation among his admirers was undimmed by later revelations about his private life; and, although neither of his brothers, Bobby and Teddy, fulfilled their ambitions of reaching the Oval Office, they kept the magic of the Kennedy name alive.

VIETNAM

The U.S. involvement in Vietnam was the American frontline in the war against communism in the 1960s, when few Americans dissented from the Kennedy worldview that saw U.S. vigilance as the chief bulwark against the spread of Soviet and Chinese-inspired communism. Whether Kennedy would have continued that strategy if he had lived has been widely debated. After Kennedy's assassination his successor, Lyndon B. Johnson, announced that he would not let South Vietnam go the way of China and become communist, and the stage was set. For the United States, Vietnam was the place where the Cold War finally became hot.

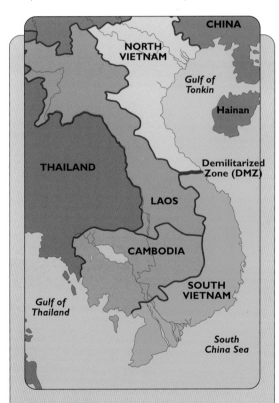

TROOP LEVELS IN VIETNAM

By mid-1962, the U.S. had established the United States Military Assistance Command, Vietnam, led by General Paul D. Harkins. By the end of 1962, there were more than 12,000 U.S. military personnel (Air Force, Army Special Forces or "Green Berets," Marines, and Navy) advising and working with their South Vietnamese counterparts. An 18-man U.S. Marine contingent worked with the South Vietnamese Marine Corps (VNMC), as well as a Marine helicopter task group, codenamed Shu Fly, comprising a helicopter squadron and support elements. By the end of 1964, the United States Military Assistance Command, under General Westmoreland, had grown to a presence of more than 20,000 troops.

During the 1960s, the United States and the Soviet Union competed in an arms race in order to secure supremacy of weaponry over their counterpart. During the 1960 presidential campaign, John F. Kennedy made much of a supposed "missile gap," alleging that the Soviets had a decisive lead in this type of weaponry. Kennedy was wrong, but before he left office in January 1961, President Eisenhower had already more than doubled the U.S. military's missile research budget. Later that year, Kennedy increased the overall defense budget by more than 20 percent, to about 60 percent of total federal expenditure. Across the 1960s, the U.S. defense budget rose from $45 billion to $78 billion by 1970, while it is estimated that Soviet expenditure kept pace, up from $37 billion to $72 billion in the same period.

The possibility that the two superpowers might devastate Europe while their own homelands remained unharmed had little appeal for many Europeans. This was one reason why, in 1960, the French tested their first atomic bomb and decided to keep independent control over whether to use nuclear weapons in any future conflict. Britain, too, had built its own nuclear weapons in the 1950s and then modernized them with U.S. assistance during the 1960s. Elsewhere, the Soviet Union's fellow communist power, China, tested its first nuclear weapon in 1964.

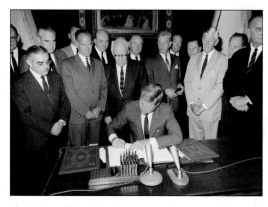

The signing of the Limited Test Ban Treaty was a sign that the United States and the Soviet Union realized they must do their utmost to prevent a nuclear confrontation.

On August 6, 1963, after more than eight years of negotiations, the United States, Britain, and the Soviet Union signed the Limited Nuclear Test Ban Treaty.

The Treaty prohibited nuclear weapons tests or explosions underwater, in the atmosphere, or in outer space; allowed underground nuclear tests as long as no radioactive debris fell outside the boundaries of the nation conducting the test; and pledged the signatories to work toward complete disarmament, an end to the arms race, and an end to the contamination of the environment by radioactive substances.

Following the peaceful resolution of the Cuban Missile Crisis in October 1962, President Kennedy and Premier Khrushchev now sought to reduce tensions between their two nations. Both leaders realized they had come dangerously close to nuclear war. As Nikita Khrushchev described it, "The two most powerful nations had been squared off against each other, each with its finger on the button." Kennedy shared this concern, once remarking at a White House meeting, "It is insane that two men, sitting on opposite sides of the world, should be able to decide to bring an end to civilization."

POLARIS

Polaris was the name of a missile system developed by the U.S. Navy for deployment in its nuclear-armed submarines. The first Polaris submarine came into service in 1960 and test-fired its first missile (with a range of more than 1,200 miles/1,920 km) the same year. Each submarine carried 16 missiles combining more destructive power than all the bombs dropped in World War II. Longer-range versions of Polaris came into service later in the 1960s, and in 1970 were joined by a new missile, Poseidon, with multiple warheads. The Soviet Union did not manage to build a system equivalent to Polaris until 1967–1968, by which time the U.S. Navy had 41 Polaris submarines in service.

Military strategists called submarine missiles like Polaris "second-strike" weapons. They could not be aimed quite accurately enough or carry the massive warheads needed to smash missile bases or other military installations on land; but, because the ocean is so vast, they would be virtually impossible to hunt down and destroy before they had a chance to fire their missiles with incalculable effect in time of war. In the deadly calculations of mutual assured destruction, Polaris was the ideal system. Polaris submarines would be guaranteed to survive an enemy "first strike," but could not themselves be used successfully in such an attack. They were designed for deterrence and, it was hoped, were never to be used.

CTBT

The Comprehensive Nuclear Test Ban Treaty (CTBT) banned all nuclear explosions in all environments for military or civilian purposes. The Treaty was opened for signature in New York on September 24, 1996, when it was signed by 71 states, including five of the eight then nuclear-capable states. The CTBT has now been signed by 177 states and ratified by 138. However, within the context of the Cold War, skepticism in the capability to verify compliance with a comprehensive nuclear test ban treaty posed a major obstacle to any agreement.

THE KENNEDY ASSASSINATION

Since President John F. Kennedy was assassinated in Dallas, Texas, on November 22, 1963, conspiracy theories have abounded that Lee Harvey Oswald did not act alone in Kennedy's murder. Many believed that the murder of Oswald two days after the assassination proved it. Why had it been so easy for Mafia member Jack Ruby to kill Oswald? Did Ruby's action not suggest there were people who wanted Oswald silenced?

The Warren Commission, tasked with finding the truth, gave rise to further doubts. In 1976, a committee of the House of Representatives conducted a review of the Warren Report, and found that there was a "high probability" that a second gunman had fired at the president.

If there had been a conspiracy, the two prime candidates were the government of Cuba and the Mafia. Fidel Castro had repeatedly claimed that the CIA was attempting to assassinate him, and Oswald had visited Havana just before the assassination. However, no evidence has ever shown that Kennedy fell victim to a foreign communist plot, and the select committee did not find that any foreign or internal U.S. agency was implicated in the assassination.

LEE HARVEY OSWALD

Lee Harvey Oswald, who was born in 1939, had the sort of childhood that often leads a young man into crime. His father died when he was two, and his mother subsequently entered into two unsuccessful marriages. Shortly after the death of his father, Lee was placed for a brief period in an orphanage in New Orleans, his birthplace. After his mother remarried, Lee was returned to her and from 1945 to 1952 was shunted around various cities in Texas and Louisiana. In 1952, he moved with his mother (now divorced from her second husband) to New York. Although Lee scored a high mark of 118 on an intelligence test, his school record was poor, and he was a frequent truant. He became increasingly moody and withdrawn, a form of maladjustment that a school psychiatrist attributed to parental neglect.

Lee Harvey Oswald left school at the age of 18 and joined the U.S. Marines, where he became a skilled sharpshooter. He was released from the Marines in 1959 on grounds of ill health and later that year he went to Moscow, where he asked to renounce his U.S. citizenship and applied for (but was not given) Soviet citizenship. In 1962, he told the U.S. consulate in Moscow that he had "seen the light" and returned to the United States with a Russian wife, Marina, and a baby daughter. He took to describing himself as a Marxist and joined the pro-Castro Fair Play for Cuba Committee in New Orleans. After failing to get a visa to Cuba, he nevertheless visited Havana, entering Cuba from Mexico in September 1963. In October, he was hired by the Texas School Book Depository. The FBI had a considerable file on Oswald, but its director, J. Edgar Hoover, concluded months before the assassination of President John F. Kennedy that he did not present a threat "to the personal safety of the president."

The motorcade carrying President Kennedy begins its fateful journey in sparkling sunshine at Dallas airport on the morning of November 22, 1963.

GULF OF TONKIN INCIDENT

U.S. President Lyndon B. Johnson was determined that his country would not be intimidated by North Vietnamese aggression in international waters, and responded accordingly.

On August 2, 1964, in international waters off the North Vietnamese coast, the USS *Maddox* was attacked by three North Vietnamese torpedo boats. One sprayed the Maddox with machine-gun fire. Aircraft from the USS *Ticonderoga*, then in the Gulf of Tonkin, responded to the attack and the *Maddox* retreated. Two days later, on August 4, the *Maddox*, now joined by the USS *C. Turner Joy*, was again attacked by North Vietnamese naval boats. When the *Maddox*'s sonar detected enemy torpedoes having been fired, both U.S. ships took evasive action and opened fire, sinking one, possibly two, of the North Vietnamese boats.

GULF OF TONKIN RESOLUTION

A resolution was put before the U.S. Congress by President Johnson on August 5, 1964, in reaction to two allegedly unprovoked attacks by North Vietnamese torpedo boats on the destroyers *Maddox* and *C. Turner Joy* of the U.S. 7th Fleet in the Gulf of Tonkin on August 2 and August 4, respectively. Its purpose was to approve and support the determination of the president, as commander-in-chief, in taking all necessary measures to repel any armed attack against the forces of the United States and to prevent any further aggression. It also declared that the maintenance of international peace and security in Southeast Asia was vital to U.S. interests and world peace. Both houses of Congress passed the resolution on August 7, the Representatives by 414 votes to 0, and the Senate by 88 to 2. The resolution was the principal constitutional authorization for the escalation of U.S. military involvement in the Vietnam War. Several years later, when the U.S. public became disillusioned with the war in Vietnam, many Congressmen saw the resolution as giving the president a blanket power to wage war, and it was repealed in 1970. In 1995, Vo Nguyen Giap, North Vietnam's military commander during the war, admitted the August 2 attack on the USS *Maddox* but denied the attack of August 4, which the Johnson administration had cited.

THE DOMINICAN REPUBLIC

The Dominican Republic's dictator, Rafael Trujillo, had ruled the Caribbean country since 1930 until his assassination in 1961. He had become increasingly unpopular in the 1950s for his use of fear and torture to maintain his grip on power. He was murdered by being shot to death in an ambush organized by his political rivals.

As a result, late in 1962, the Dominican Republic held its first free elections in 38 years. The winner was writer and academic Juan Bosch, who had spent many years in exile from his homeland. Bosch was inaugurated as president of the Dominican Republic on February 27, 1963, and set out to establish

WHY THE U.S. INTERVENED

While it was true that there were communists and Fidelistas—followers of Fidel Castro—among the rebels in the Dominican Republic, they were by no means the dominant element, and it was an exaggeration to claim that the revolution was communist-inspired. However, the details of the civil war did not interest the U.S. president, Lyndon B. Johnson. He simply realized that no president would be reelected if he allowed a second Cuba to appear in the Caribbean.

Johnson had another motive as well. The crisis arose just as a huge U.S. troop buildup in Vietnam was getting underway. Johnson's intervention in the Dominican Republic was designed to show the North Vietnamese that the U.S. had the strength to invade a small country and was prepared to use it. The massive show of force—far more than the strength of fighting factions in the Dominican Republic justified—was meant to intimidate North Vietnam's leader, Ho Chi Minh, and to bring him to the negotiating table. It failed to do so.

The intervention of the United States led to the death of some 2,000 Dominicans; thousands more were injured. However, even if the civil war did not warrant the deployment of such overwhelming U.S. firepower, the people of the Dominican Republic did reap benefits. Under Balaguer, there were strong economic gains and some social reforms. Following the intervention, the Dominican Republic managed to sustain democracy, even though corruption remained rife and the economy weak.

an administration dedicated to maintaining democratic freedoms. Bosch had little idea of the powerful forces ranged against him, such as the country's major landowners and wealthy industrialists, who felt he was offering too much power to the workers. The military, who had previously enjoyed some autonomy, also began to feel that Bosch was placing too many restrictions upon them. In addition, left-wing activists began to stir up the urban unemployed, leaving the capital city, Santo Domingo, in a constant state of unrest.

This backdrop gave the conservative upper classes and their military supporters the excuse to stage a bloodless coup. Bosch was forced into exile in Puerto Rico, and the country was run by a three-man junta. However, on April 24, 1965, a group of young military officers rebelled, with the aim of restoring the democratically elected Bosch government. The action precipitated a civil war.

U.S. troops go in

The pro-Bosch forces were on the point of winning, when the U.S. Embassy in the capital reported back to the government in Washington, D.C., that there were communist sympathizers within the ranks of the Bosch faction. Fearing another Cuba, on April 28, 1963, President Lyndon B. Johnson sent in U.S. troops, ostensibly to protect and evacuate U.S. citizens but in reality to try to halt the rebels' advance. The U.S. Marines met little resistance, although troops guarding the U.S. Embassy exchanged fire with snipers. By the middle of May, U.S. troop strength in the country had reached 23,500, more than seven times the estimated number of Dominicans under arms.

Under pressure from the United States, the Organization of American States (OAS) belatedly sanctioned the intervention, and military command was handed over to an Inter-American Peace Force (IAPF). Small units comprising Hondurans, Guatemalans, Paraguayans, and Costa Ricans, and, later, a larger contingent of Brazilians, joined the U.S. forces. Fresh elections were held in 1966, when Bosch was defeated by Joaquin Balaguer, a conservative who had served as president under Trujillo. Balaguer managed to unite the country and was reelected to office in 1970.

Soon after the establishment of the People's Republic, China's leader, Mao Zedong, traveled to Moscow to negotiate the 1950 Sino–Soviet Treaty of Friendship, Alliance, and Mutual Assistance. Under the agreement, China gave the Soviet Union certain rights, such as the continued use of a naval base at Luda, Liaoning Province, in return for military support, weapons, and large amounts of economic aid and technological assistance, including technical advisers and machinery.

During the second half of the 1950s, strains in the Sino–Soviet alliance gradually began to emerge over questions of ideology, security, and economic development. Chinese leaders were disturbed by the Soviet Union's Nikita Khrushchev's move toward deStalinization and peaceful coexistence with the West. In addition to ideological disagreements, Beijing was dissatisfied with several aspects of the Sino–Soviet security relationship, especially Soviet reluctance to honor an agreement to provide nuclear-weapons technology to China. Eventually, Moscow withdrew all Soviet advisers from China in 1960. The Sino–Soviet dispute was also intensified by increasing competition between Beijing and Moscow for influence in the Third World and in the international communist movement.

CHINA'S NUCLEAR WEAPONS

In 1951 China signed a secret agreement with the Soviet Union under which China provided uranium ores in exchange for Soviet assistance in the nuclear field. In mid-October 1957, the Chinese and Soviets signed another agreement on new technology for national defense that included provision for additional Soviet nuclear assistance, as well as the furnishing of some surface-to-surface and surface-to-air missiles. The Soviet Union also agreed to supply China with a sample atomic bomb and to provide technical assistance in the manufacture of nuclear weapons.

When Sino–Soviet relations cooled in the late 1950s and early 1960s, the Soviet Union withheld plans and data for an atomic bomb, abrogated the agreement on transferring defense technology, and began the withdrawal of Soviet advisers in 1960. Despite the termination of Soviet assistance, China committed itself to continue nuclear weapons' development to break "the superpowers' monopoly on nuclear weapons," to ensure Chinese security against Soviet and U.S. threats, and to increase Chinese prestige and power internationally.

China made remarkable progress in the 1960s in developing nuclear weapons. In a 32-month period, China successfully exploded its first atomic bomb (October 16, 1964), launched its first nuclear missile (October 25, 1966), and detonated its first hydrogen bomb (June 14, 1967). By the end of 1970, China had fabricated around 200 nuclear weapons. The country had joined the international nuclear club.

INDONESIAN COUP

Indonesia became a key battleground between East and West in the mid-1960s. The country had been ruled by its first president, Sukarno, for more than 20 years. He had helped win Indonesia's independence from the Netherlands in 1945, but, by the early 1960s, his position depended on balancing the demands of the opposing and increasingly hostile forces of the army and the Indonesian Communist Party (PKI). By 1965, the PKI had penetrated all levels of Sukarno's government and had gained influence at the expense of the army. The army itself had become divided between a PKI-allied left-wing, and a right-wing that was being courted by Western countries.

Bloodshed in a large scale

On September 30, 1965, six of the military's most senior officers were executed in an attempted coup by the so-called "30 September Movement," a group from within the armed forces. Within a few hours, Major General Suharto took control of the army and defeated the coup. Anticommunists, following the army's lead, then went on a violent purge of communists, killing an estimated half million people and destroying the PKI, which was blamed for the coup.

In March 1967, the Indonesian parliament (MPRS) named General Suharto as acting president of Indonesia. He was formally appointed president one year later. As a result of his elimination of the communists, Suharto was seen as a pro-Western and anticommunist political force. This cemented the military and diplomatic relationship between Indonesia and the Western powers, leading to American, British, and Australian arms sales and military training.

THE MALAYAN EMERGENCY

The communist insurrection in Malaya from 1948 to 1960 posed a challenge not only to the British imperial regime, but also to a peaceful political transition to Malayan independence. After a faltering start, the British realized that the way to defeat the communists was to address the underlying economic, social, and political problems facing the Chinese community while, at the same time, bringing government control to the fringe areas from where the Malayan Communist Party (MCP) received much of its popular support. The successful "hearts and minds" campaign that the British employed destroyed support for the communists and ensured that Malaya would become a democratic country after its independence in August 1957.

THE SIX-DAY WAR

From its establishment in 1948, Israel had been in a state of war with its Arab neighbors. A turning point was reached in May 1967, when the Israeli prime minister, Levi Eshkol, sought to ward off border raids by the Syrian-backed guerrilla organization Al Fatah. On June 5, Israel launched a preemptive strike against its three main enemies, Syria, Egypt, and Jordan, who had formed an anti-Israeli defensive pact.

In one day, Israel destroyed the air forces of Syria, Egypt, and Jordan, and followed up by occupying the Arab quarter of Jerusalem on June 7. On the same day, Egyptian troops in the Sinai Peninsula were scattered by Israeli forces, which reached the Suez Canal. Israeli armies also occupied the West Bank of the Jordan River and the Golan Heights in Syria. On June 10, the United Nations secured a ceasefire, effectively enabling Israel to keep all its territorial gains. The conflict had no great effect on the Cold War. The Soviets had contemplated military intervention on behalf of their Arab allies, but the risk of nuclear war with the U.S. dissuaded them.

SOVIET AID TO EGYPT

After the Six-Day War, small-scale hostilities continued between the Arab nations and Israel. By January 1970, for example, Israeli planes were flying at will over eastern Egypt. To remedy this politically intolerable situation, Egyptian president Abdel Nasser flew to Moscow and asked the Soviet Union to establish an air defense system manned by Soviet pilots and antiaircraft forces protected by Soviet troops. To obtain Soviet aid, Nasser had to grant the Soviet Union control over a number of Egyptian airfields, as well as operational control over a large part of the Egyptian army. The Soviet Union sent between 10,000 and 15,000 troops and advisers to Egypt, and Soviet pilots flew combat missions. A screen of surface-to-air missiles (SAMs) was set up, and Soviet pilots joined Egyptian aircrews in patrolling Egyptian air space.

Soviet influence in Egypt: Egyptian president Anwar el-Sadat (right) with Alexander Shelepin, a member of the KGB, the Soviet spy service. Sadat became president in 1970.

THE ANTIWAR MOVEMENT

By 1967, opposition to the Vietnam War had split American society. On the weekend of April 15-16, 1967, 125,000 antiwar demonstrators gathered in New York, with another 5,000 in San Francisco as part of the "Spring Mobilization to End the War in Vietnam." On October 21, 1967, some 50,000 demonstrators marched on the Pentagon. There was a dramatic erosion in support for the war in the aftermath of the Tet Offensive in Vietnam in January 1968.

The protests began to take a more violent turn as one antiwar group, Students for a Democratic Society (SDS), grew increasingly militant. By 1969, it had split into several factions, the most notorious of which was the Weather Underground, which began planting bombs. Over 5,000 bombs went off in all. In May 1970, a protest at Kent State University against U.S. incursion into the territory of Vietnam's neighbor, Cambodia, ended in bloodshed when the Ohio National Guard opened fire on the protesters, leaving four dead.

Protests against the Vietnam War had also spread around the world. In May 1965, 50 demonstrators were arrested in Sydney, Australia, just days after Australia had increased its contingent fighting in Vietnam to 1,300. Antiwar feeling also ran particularly high in Britain. On July 4, 1965, a demonstration was held in London's Trafalgar Square. That night, a homemade bomb exploded against the back door of the American Express offices in the Haymarket area of the city, less than half a mile away. In October 1965, two days of protests in London led to a march on the U.S. Embassy in Grosvenor Square, where 78 demonstrators were arrested. In 1968, Grosvenor Square was also the scene of a full-scale antiwar riot.

U.S. Defense Secretary Robert McNamara warned of the great damage the Vietnam War was doing to America's image abroad. In his resignation letter in 1968, McNamara wrote: "The picture of the world's greatest superpower killing or seriously injuring 1,000 noncombatants a week, while trying to pound a tiny backward nation into submission on an issue whose merits are hotly disputed is not a pretty one." It could have come straight from an antiwar leaflet.

A large antiwar demonstration held in Washington, D.C. The antiwar movement embraced many groups, from violent left-wing activists to genuine pacifists.

HANOI'S STRATEGY

By the late 1960s, the North Vietnamese had come to view the antiwar demonstrations in the United States and the coverage of the war on U.S. television as part of their strategy to win the war. One of the first U.S. politicians to realize this reality was Secretary of Defense Robert McNamara. A business graduate and political pragmatist, in 1967 McNamara had instigated a detailed analysis of enemy engagements by the Defense Departments Systems Analysis Office.

The report stated that the North Vietnamese and their Viet Cong allies in the south "started the shooting in over 90 percent of company-sized firefights," and that "over 80 percent began with a well-organized enemy attack." It continued: "Since their losses rise—as in the first quarter of 1967—and fall—as they have done since—with their choice of whether to fight or not, they can probably hold their losses to about 2,000 a week, regardless of our force level. If their strategy is to wait us out, they will control their losses to a level low enough to be sustained indefinitely, but high enough to tempt us to increase our forces to the point of U.S. public rejection." Given the growing protests on the streets of America, McNamara concluded the North Vietnamese strategy was working, and that U.S. withdrawal from the war was inevitable.

THE TET OFFENSIVE

The Tet Offensive was a major military campaign carried out between January and September 1968 by forces of the Viet Cong, or National Front for the Liberation of South Vietnam, and the North Vietnamese Army, or People's Army of Vietnam. The purpose of the offensive was to strike hard at the military and civilian command and control centers of the Republic of Vietnam (South Vietnam), the United States, and their allies. With carefully planned and simultaneous attacks on strongholds throughout South Vietnam, North Vietnamese commanders hoped to spark a general uprising among the population that would lead to the toppling of the Saigon government.

The operations are known as "the Tet Offensive" because they began in the early hours of Tet, the most important Vietnamese holiday, which celebrates the first day of the year on a traditional lunar calendar. Both North and South Vietnam announced on national radio broadcasts that there would be a three-day ceasefire in honor of Tet.

However, a wave of Viet Cong attacks began on the morning of January 30 in the I and II Corps Tactical Zones. When the main communist military operation began the next morning (the 31st), it quickly became clear that the offensive was countrywide in scope and was well coordinated, with more than 80,000 Viet Cong troops striking at more than 100 towns and cities, including 36 of 44 provincial capitals, 5 of the 6 autonomous cities, 72 of 245 district towns, and also the national capital, Saigon. The Tet Offensive was the largest military operation conducted by either side up to that point in the Vietnam War.

CHINESE AID TO NORTH VIETNAM

The military support provided by the People's Republic of China (which included advisers, equipment, and combat troops) was a decisive factor in the ultimate North Vietnamese victory in the Vietnam War. The supply of small arms, mortars, ammunition, uniforms, tanks, artillery, radars, antiaircraft guns, jet aircraft, trucks, and naval vessels were critical in the North Vietnamese struggle. For example, there were thousands of Chinese antiaircraft artillery troops in North Vietnam, peaking at a total of 17 divisions and 150,000 men in 1967. In addition, the Chinese promise to intervene with massive numbers of troops in the event of an invasion of North Vietnam effectively eliminated this course of action as one of the potential war-winning options for the West.

The initial attacks by North Vietnamese forces stunned the U.S. military and its allies, taking them completely by surprise. However, most of the advances were quickly driven back, and, in so doing, the Allies inflicted huge casualties on the enemy. Only in two places did the fighting last more than a few days: around the the city of Hue, where combat went on for a month, and at the U.S. combat base of Khe Sanh, where fighting went on for two months.

Overall, the Tet Offensive was disastrous for North Vietnam, as it was beaten decisively and quickly in most areas. However, for the U.S. government and for the U.S. public Tet was a shock, as they had believed that the North was incapable of such a campaign.

A Czech youth attempts to stop a Soviet tank following the Warsaw Pact invasion of Czechoslovakia in August 1968. The youth was later shot and killed by Russian troops.

In the 1960s, the Czechoslovak economy became severely stagnated, and on January 5, 1968, Alexander Dubcek, a moderate reformer, became Czech leader. He steered the reform movement toward liberalism, lifting censorship and seeking to democratize socialism. His efforts took on a new, popular dynamism in the spring of 1968, and the Soviet leadership became alarmed. In mid-July, a Warsaw Pact conference was held without Czechoslovakia. The assembled nations declared the defense of Czechoslovakia's socialist principles to be the task of all Warsaw Pact member states.

On August 3, delegates from the Soviet Union, East Germany, Czechoslovakia, Poland, Hungary, and Bulgaria met to sign the Bratislava Declaration, affirming their fidelity to Marxism-Leninism and declaring an implacable struggle against "bourgeois" ideology and all "antisocialist" forces. On August 20, Warsaw Pact tanks and troops entered Czechoslovakia, and Dubcek and his government were arrested.

ALEXANDER DUBCEK

Alexander Dubcek (1921-1992) was a member of the Czech Communist Party who had fought the Germans during World War II. A hugely popular figure in the 1960s, after the Warsaw Pact invasion of Czechoslovakia in 1968, he gave a speech in Prague, breaking into tears as he told his people that much of what they had achieved was lost. After April 1969, Dubcek was demoted, expelled from the party, and eventually sent into internal exile as a forestry official. He could talk to no one outside his family without permission. In November 1989, as part of the country's "Velvet Revolution," he spoke at a rally in Bratislava and later stood on the balcony overlooking Wenceslas Square in Prague with newly elected President Vaclav Havel while crowds cheered. Dubcek was unanimously elected chairman of the Federal Assembly on December 28, 1989, and reelected in 1990. Dubcek died at the age of 70 on November 7, 1992, from injuries sustained in a car crash.

Since its inception in 1945, the United Nations (UN) has been a forum for top-level debate and diplomacy. Its purpose was to reduce international tensions and work for world peace. However, the UN often found itself a mere pawn in the Cold War between the United States and the Soviet Union. The superpowers came to a tacit agreement, for instance, that neither would interfere within each other's "sphere of influence," an understanding that would, in many ways, undermine the efforts of the UN in many future wars.

The power of veto

The United States had a great advantage over the Soviet Union, which found itself isolated against the four other anticommunist nations with permanent seats on the UN Security Council. Not until 1970 did the United States use its power of veto, by which time the Soviet Union had used its 112 times. The veto was of more symbolic than real importance. Whenever either of the superpowers disliked a UN resolution, they ignored it.

In the 1960s, the UN showed that it was better equipped to police peace settlements than to prevent war from breaking out in the first place. Its mandate did not run everywhere, however. After the United States, ignoring the charters of both the UN and the Organization of American States (OAS), invaded the Dominican Republic in 1965 to put down a rebellion, the UN found its attempt to mediate in the dispute overshadowed by the presence of the OAS, which asserted a superior right to deal with a crisis in its own region. However, in sending peacekeeping forces to the Middle East and to the Congo and Cyprus in the early 1960s, the UN established precedents for the future.

UNITED NATIONS' MEMBERSHIP

By the early 1960s, the United Nations' Security Council had become unrepresentative of the General Assembly. In 1945, there were a total of 51 member-nations in the United Nations. The admission of newly independent nations from Asia and, above all, Africa increased the membership to 100 by the end of 1960, and to 126 by the end of 1970. Pressure from those new nations resulted in an increase in the size of the Security Council from 11 to 15 members in 1963. At the same time, it was agreed that, from 1966, the Council should always have five nations from Africa and Asia combined, and two from Latin America. Yet Latin America, Africa, and Asia still had no representative (apart from Taiwan) with permanent membership of the Security Council.

THE SPACE RACE

On May 25, 1961, President John F. Kennedy said that America should "commit itself to achieving the goal, before the decade is out, of landing a man on the moon." Although the Soviets denied it, they were planning to do the same. The space race had begun.

In 1966, the U.S. spent nearly $3 billion on the Apollo space program. However, in February 1967, the Soviets made the first landing on the moon with Luna 9. Two months later, Luna 10 became the moon's first artificial satellite. However, Apollo 7—the first manned flight in the U.S. Apollo program—made a successful 163-orbit test flight in October 1968, and the go-ahead was then given for Apollo 8's trip to orbit the moon.

While Apollo 9 was successfully testing a lunar module, the Soviets responded with tests on probes intended to fly to the moon to scoop up dust and return it to Earth—taking the edge off NASA's planned manned landing, which had the same aim. However, the first two Soviet "moonscooper" launches—in April and June 1969—failed to leave Earth's orbit. In May 1969, Apollo 10 then swooped to within 10 miles (16 km) of the lunar surface.

The Apollo 11 moon landing signaled to the world that the Soviets had lost the space race.

APOLLO MOON LANDING

When Neil Armstrong stepped out of Apollo 11 onto the surface of the moon on July 20, 1969, it was clear that the Soviets had lost the space race. American organization and technology had proved superior. Part of the success was due to the fact that the U.S. had been able to devote far more money to the venture. Apollo's budget had been $24 billion, while the Soviets had spent just $4.5 billion. The moon landing was the most spectacular propaganda victory for the United States. To many in the West, it demonstrated the superiority of democracy over communism.

VIETNAMIZATION

Despite attempts to establish peace in Vietnam and a halt to the U.S. bombing campaign, the North Vietnamese Army (NVA) continued to seek victory on the battlefield. Traffic increased along the NVA's supply route, the Ho Chi Minh Trail, and 1969 began with a major NVA offensive. In January, several South Vietnamese cities came under rocket and artillery attack. Infantry assaults began in February, and Saigon also came under attack. In March 1969, U.S. president Richard Nixon threatened to resume bombing raids.

Meanwhile, Richard Nixon's new policy was to be the "Vietnamization" of the war. U.S. troops would be gradually withdrawn, while the newly reequipped South Vietnamese Army (ARVN) would take over their battlefield duties. Some 25,000 U.S. troops would pull out at once. In July 1969, Nixon also unveiled the "Nixon Doctrine," ruling out U.S. engagement in any future Vietnam-style wars in Asia. At the same time, he began the secret bombing of Cambodia.

South Vietnamese troops battle North Vietnamese Army (NVA) forces in a South Vietnamese town. In general the ARVN fared poorly against the battle-hardened NVA.

Communist forces kept up the pressure in Vietnam, despite the death of Ho Chi Minh in September 1969. President Thieu attempted to sue for peace by offering elections that would include the NLF. However, Vice President Ky warned that any attempt to form a coalition with the NLF would result in another military coup.

U.S. TROOP LEVELS IN VIETNAM

On October 15, 1969, Nixon made a televised speech promising an "orderly scheduled timetable" for U.S. troop withdrawals from Vietnam. His announcement did little to quell public feeling. Two weeks later, 250,000 people attended an antiwar demonstration in Washington, D.C. Despite continuing troop withdrawals, U.S. casualties in the war continued to rise, topping 40,000 by the end of 1969. Nevertheless, U.S. troop levels in Vietnam did steadily decrease, from 536,100 in 1968, to 475,200 in 1969, and then down to 4,200 by 1972.

The Nuclear Non-Proliferation Treaty was signed in 1968 by several major nuclear and nonnuclear powers (United States, Britain, the Soviet Union) as well as 59 other countries. It pledged to halt the spread of nuclear technology, and, although it did not ultimately prevent nuclear proliferation, for advocates of arms control the treaty was a success within the context of the Cold War arms race and deep concern about the global consequences of nuclear war, as it set a precedent for international cooperation between nuclear and nonnuclear states to prevent proliferation. Still, the treaty had one major drawback in that two nuclear powers, France and the People's Republic of China, did not sign the agreement.

The signing of the Nuclear Non-Proliferation Treaty in July 1968. The treaty was designed to prevent the further spread of nuclear weapons and encourage negotiations on nuclear arms control.

U.S. AND SOVIET NUCLEAR MISSILES

The U.S. Minuteman II missile was first tested in 1964 and was put into service from 1966. Some 500 were eventually built and deployed in underground silos in the western United States. This missile carried a 1.1-megaton warhead, and its accuracy was such that half of those fired, it was predicted, would detonate within 500 yards (460 m) of their target. The Minuteman II was capable of storing data on eight potential targets, with one being selected just prior to launch. It operated on solid fuel and so could be launched at short notice. It had a range of 7,000 miles (11,200 km) and was built by the Boeing company.

Soviet missiles included the slightly earlier SS-9 Scarp. The first version of this type was initially deployed in 1966, with 288, in several versions, eventually being built and positioned in underground silos. The Scarp used liquid fuel, but, unlike in some earlier missiles, it could be stored aboard the missile. Previous types using nonstorable fuel could take several hours to make ready for firing. The Scarp's warhead is thought to have been of between 12 and 20 megatons in yield, with half of those fired being expected to strike within 1,000 yards (950 m) of their target. The different versions were reported to have ranges from 4,500 to 6,500 miles (7,200 to 10,400 km).

The global balance of power in the Cold War had been tilting in Moscow's favor through most of the 1970s. The United States had acknowledged strategic parity with the Soviet Union in the SALT I treaty, while the Soviets had claimed the right, through the Brezhnev Doctrine, to resist all challenges to Marxism–Leninism wherever they might occur. Despite U.S. success in excluding the Soviets from the Egyptian-Israeli peace negotiations, the 1973 war triggered an Arab oil embargo, followed by price increases that would hurt Western economies for the remainder of the decade. Meanwhile, the Soviet Union, a major oil exporter, was raking in huge profits and could afford to increase military spending, at a time when the United States defense budget was being cut in half.

U.S. problems in the 1970s

Americans seemed mired in endless internal debates, first over the Vietnam War, then Watergate, then, during Jimmy Carter's presidency, over charges that he had failed to protect allies such as the Shah of Iran or Anastasio Somoza, the Nicaraguan dictator whose government fell to the Marxist Sandinistas in the summer of 1979. The low point came in November of that year, when Iranians invaded the U.S. Embassy in Tehran, taking more than 90 people hostage. This humiliation, closely followed by the Soviet invasion of Afghanistan, made it seem as though Washington was on the defensive while Moscow was on the advance.

However, in reality the Soviet Union and its Warsaw Pact allies were on the decline. One hint of this came as early as March 1970, when, in a spirit of diplomacy, the East German authorities invited West German Chancellor Willy Brandt to visit Erfurt, unwisely giving him a hotel room with a window overlooking a public square. To their intense embarrassment, hundreds of East Germans gathered to cheer their visitor: "[T]he preparation for the Erfurt meeting," party officials later admitted, "was not fully recognized as a key component in the class conflict between socialism and imperialism."

A North Vietnamese tank crashes through the gates of Saigon's presidential palace, signaling the fall of South Vietnam to communism in 1975.

More serious signs of discontent arose in Poland the following December, when protests over food prices led the army to kill dozens of striking workers in Gdansk and Gdynia. Very significantly, this crisis did not lead Moscow to invoke the Brezhnev Doctrine: instead the Soviet leadership ordered an increase in the production of consumer goods, and it approved imports of food and technology from Western Europe and the United States. This made stability in the region contingent not on the use of military force but rather on the willingness of capitalists to extend credit, a striking vulnerability for Marxist-Leninist regimes.

Crisis in the Warsaw Pact

The Soviet oil windfall had a downside. The Soviet Union chose to pass along price increases to the Eastern Europeans, leading to a doubling of their oil costs within a year. While not as big as the increases faced by the West, the unanticipated rise in expenses undercut the improvements in living standards Moscow had hoped for. Meanwhile, swelling oil revenues were diminishing incentives for Soviet planners to make their own economy more productive. It was no source of strength for the Soviet Union to be sustaining a defense burden that may well have been three times that of the United States by the end of the 1970s, when its gross domestic product was only about one-sixth the size of its U.S. counterpart.

From this perspective, the Soviet Union's support for Marxist revolutionaries in Africa, its SS-20 missile deployment, and its invasion of Afghanistan look less like a coordinated strategy to shift the global balance of power and more like the absence of any strategy at all. Major cracks were emerging in the Soviet empire, plus many contradictions. For example, its leadership committed itself to the defense of human rights—as at Helsinki in 1975—but was then surprised when its own citizens claimed such rights for themselves. In reality, the Soviet Union under Leonid Brezhnev's faltering rule had become incapable of performing the most fundamental task of any effective strategy: the efficient use of the available means to accomplish chosen ends. That left the field open for leaders elsewhere who more capable.

U.S. INCURSIONS INTO CAMBODIA

Between April 29 and July 22, 1970, troops of the South Vietnamese Army (ARVN) and the U.S. Army conducted a number of massive search-and-destroy operations in a dozen areas in Vietnam's neighboring country of Cambodia. The purpose of the campaign was to confront and defeat around 40,000 troops of the People's Army of Vietnam (PAVN) and the National Front for the Liberation of South Vietnam (known as the Viet Cong), which were based in the eastern part of Cambodia, adjacent to II, III, and IV Corps Tactical Zones in South Vietnam. From their bases in Cambodia, North Vietnamese troops could launch attacks at will, and the U.S. military command was determined to wipe out this constant threat. In tandem with the planned ground operations on these North Vietnamese military sanctuaries in Cambodia, a U.S.–South Vietnamese naval task force would sweep up the Mekong Delta in order to reopen a secure supply line to Phnom Penh, the Cambodian capital.

However, Cambodia was technically neutral in the Vietnam War and so incursions into its territory by U.S.-

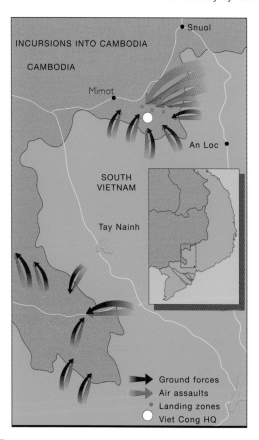

INCURSIONS INTO CAMBODIA

CAMBODIA

Snuol

Mimot

An Loc

SOUTH VIETNAM

Tay Nainh

➤ Ground forces
➤ Air assaults
• Landing zones
○ Viet Cong HQ

LAOS

In Laos the Laotian communist guerrillas, the Pathet Lao, and the NVA had been making advances in the late 1960s. U.S. president Richard Nixon responded with massive illegal B-52 raids, which created 700,000 refugees. On February 8, 1971, some 12,000 ARVN troops invaded Laos, supported by U.S. aircraft. Nixon publicly denied that U.S. troops were operating in Laos and he refused to curtail the use of U.S. air power. Congress was outraged, and Nixon's opponents tried to further limit his power to wage war. It was later admitted that U.S. troops were being sent into Laos on the pretext of rescuing downed airmen.

led forces would be controversial at home and on the international stage. Indeed, public opinion polls in May showed that only 50 percent of the U.S. public approved of President Nixon's actions.

However, after the operation was underway, Nixon also announced that several thousand U.S. troops supporting the Cambodian invasion had also entered Cambodia's "Fishhook" area bordering South Vietnam in order to attack the location of the headquarters of the communist military operation in South Vietnam. American advisers, tactical air support, medical evacuation teams, and logistical support were also part of the U.S. incursion force.

Final tally

In support of the Cambodian operation was the Vietnamese Marine Corps which, on May 9, crossed the Cambodian border and, at 09:30 hours, landed at Neck Luong to begin its phase of the operation. Allied troop numbers in Cambodia then rose to 50,000 by May 6. Withdrawal of U.S. units from Cambodia was completed when the 1st Cavalry Division (Airmobile) returned to South Vietnam on June 29.

During the U.S. and Republic of Vietnam operations in Cambodia, a reported 4,764 North Vietnamese troops were killed. In addition to this, 9,081 individual weapons, 1,283 crew-served weapons, and 5,400 tonnes (5,314 tons) of rice were captured or destroyed. These totals were exclusive of those operations that were continuing in the Parrot's Beak area, Se San Base Areas, and the Mekong River Corridor. However, in view of the massive efforts that were involved in carrying them out, the results that were achieved by the incursions into Cambodia were disappointing.

DÉTENTE

The early 1970s saw the start of a period known as "détente" (from the French word meaning "release of tensions") between the United States and the Soviet Union. The thawing of relations would probably not have happened without the simultaneous rift that developed between the communist regimes of the Soviet Union and the People's Republic of China (PRC). U.S. president Richard Nixon believed that this tension could be exploited by the United States. Secret talks with the Chinese then intimated that the United States was keen to end its isolation of the PRC.

However, all three major powers stood to gain from détente. China was fearful of the U.S.'s nuclear arsenal. The Soviet Union was spending heavily on weapons, while its people's living standards were low. Also, the Soviets were aware that their relationship with China was poor, while the United States was trying to improve relations with China. The United States was spending heavily on weapons and an easing of international tension would be of great benefit to the U.S. economy.

NIXON'S VISIT TO CHINA

In February 1972, U.S. president Richard Nixon's visit to China was the first step in formally normalizing relations between the United States and the People's Republic of China (PRC). It was the first time that a U.S. president had visited the PRC, which saw the United States as an enemy.

At the conclusion of Nixon's trip, the United States and the PRC governments issued the Shanghai Communiqué, a statement of their foreign policy views and a document that was to remain the basis of Sino-American bilateral relations for many years into the future. In the communiqué, both nations pledged to work toward the full normalization of diplomatic relations.

President Nixon (left) meets Chairman Mao of the People's Republic of China in 1972. It was the first time that a U.S. president had visited the PRC.

OSTPOLITIK

In 1970, for the first time since 1948, politicians of the Federal Republic of Germany (FRG) and the German Democratic Republic held talks, but there were no concrete results. The FRG also entered negotiations with the Soviet Union on a treaty normalizing relations. The FRG negotiators, however, insisted that any talks did not alter the West German position on future reunification of Germany. After the Soviet Union agreed, the Treaty of Moscow was signed in August 1970. The agreement opened the road to negotiations with other countries of the Soviet bloc. In December 1970, the FRG and Poland signed the Treaty of Warsaw. The treaty meant the FRG recognized Poland's western border. In return, Poland agreed to allow ethnic Germans still in Poland to emigrate to the FRG.

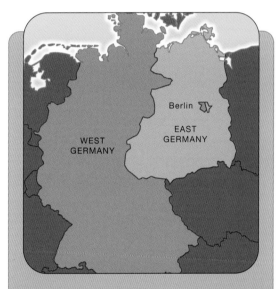

BERLIN

Concurrent with the negotiations on the treaties of Moscow and Warsaw, the four World War II allies undertook to end disagreement about the status of Berlin in talks that ultimately led to the Four Power Agreement (also known as the Quadripartite Agreement) of September 1971. The Soviet Union made two important concessions: traffic to and from West Berlin would be unimpeded in the future and, in addition, the existing ties of West Berlin to the Federal Republic of Germany (FRG) were recognized. Soviet officials, however, insisted that West Berlin was not to be considered a territory belonging to the FRG and was not to be governed by it. The Four Power Agreement charged the governments of West Berlin and the German Democratic Republic (GDR) with negotiating an accord to regulate access to and from West Berlin from the FRG and secure the right of West Berliners to visit East Berlin and the GDR. The Transit Agreement of May 1972 also secured the rights of GDR citizens to visit the FRG, but only in cases of family emergency.

Richard Nixon (left) and Leonid Brezhnev sign the SALT I Treaty in Moscow in May 1972. Behind Nixon stands future U.S. secretary of state Henry Kissinger.

"SALT" is the abbreviation given to the Strategic Arms Limitation Talks between the United States and the Soviet Union that began in 1969 and led to various treaties and agreements in the 1970s and later.

Before the SALT process started, important arms agreements had been negotiated between the United States and the USSR. They included the L mited Test Ban Treaty of 1963 and the Non-Proliferation Treaty of 1968, but these did not affect the nuclear strength of either side. SALT was meant to be different, although it would be years before the nuclear arsenal was reduced. Another important aspect of SALT was that it only concerned "strategic" arms: nuclear weapons with the longest ranges, which could strike the U.S. and Soviet homelands. Not included in the talks were tactical or battlefield nuclear weapons, which could be used as an adjunct to conventional forces, and intermediate or theater nuclear forces, such as Soviet missiles that could strike at Western Europe, for example, but that could not reach the United States itself.

SALT I & II

Strategic Arms Limitation Treaty I (SALT I) was signed in Moscow on May 26, 1972. The United States and the Soviet Union had engaged in talks from 1969 to 1972, during which they negotiated the first agreements to place limits and restraints on some of their most important armaments, such as the Anti-Ballistic Missile Treaty and the Interim Agreement on strategic offensive arms.

Strategic Arms Limitation Treaty II (SALT II) was signed in Vienna on June 18, 1979. This agreement increased limits on intercontinental ballistic missiles (ICBMs), submarine-launched ballistic missiles (SLBMs), and heavy bombers. Other limits were placed on multiple reentry vehicles and bombers with intermediate-range missiles. However, SALT II was never ratified by the two nations' legislative bodies.

THE YOM KIPPUR WAR

The Arab-Israeli wars of 1948, 1956 (at right), and 1967 (see page 38) all ended in Israeli victory. In 1973, warfare flared up again in the Middle East. On the Jewish holy day of Yom Kippur, October 6, Egypt and Syria attacked Israeli forces in Sinai on the Suez Canal and in the Golan Heights respectively. Egyptians and Syrian forces advanced quickly during the first 48 hours, breaking through the Israeli Bar-Lev Line on the Suez Canal, which was a series of fortifications and earthworks named after Israeli General Chaim Bar-Lev. Armed with the latest Soviet antitank and ground-to-air missiles, Egyptian forces were successful in inflicting heavy losses on Israeli armor and aircraft, which were only able to counterattack haphazardly. Meanwhile, similarly fierce battles developed on the Golan Heights, where 1,800 Syrian tanks were opposed by only 180 Israeli tanks and 60 artillery pieces. Syrian commandos were dropped by helicopter and captured the vital Israeli position at Jabal al Shaikh (Mount Hermon).

Egyptian defeat in the Sinai

However, early Syrian breakthroughs were driven back by the Israelis, but at the cost of heavy casualties. The turning point of the Yom Kippur War came on October 14, when the Egyptian forces attempted an over-ambitious advance into the heart of Sinai. The following day, October 15, the Israelis launched Operation Abiray-Lev ("Valiant"), a counterattack that marked a change of tactics for the Israelis, who had previously relied on air and tank support. On this occasion, Israeli infantry infiltrated the positions of the Egyptian missile and antitank batteries, which were unable to deal with ground attacks delivered with devastating speed and power. The Israeli infantry destroyed much Egyptian armor and went on to

CAMP DAVID ACCORDS

After the Yom Kippur War, much patient diplomatic work brought peace at last between Egypt and Israel in 1978. This landmark agreement was brokered by U.S. president Jimmy Carter between Israel's prime minister Menachim Begin and Egypt's president Anwar Sadat. The Camp David Accords were so-named as they were finalized at Camp David, the U.S. president's retreat in Maryland, and they were signed in Washington, D.C., on March 26, 1979. However, the key issue of the Palestinian Arabs, who were still demanding a homeland, remained unresolved.

After months of talks, the United States, South Vietnam, the Viet Cong, and North Vietnam reached an agreement to end the fighting in Vietnam. The terms of the Paris Peace Accords of January 1973 were: a ceasefire in North and South Vietnam, the withdrawal of all U.S. forces and the dismantling of all U.S. bases, the release of all prisoners, and the withdrawal of all foreign troops from Laos and Cambodia. The 17th Parallel would remain as the dividing line between North and South until Vietnam could be reunited by "peaceful means." This agreement was augmented by a second accord in June. In August 1973, Congress proscribed any further U.S. military activity in Indochina. However, North and South denounced each other for violating the truce, and fighting broke out once more.

U.S. negotiators at the Paris Peace Accords, which signaled the beginning of the end of 30 years of war in Southeast Asia.

HENRY KISSINGER

The son of German immigrants, Henry Kissinger (b. 1923) received his PhD in 1954 from Harvard University, becoming professor of government in 1962 and director of the Defense Studies Program from 1959 to 1969. He also served as a consultant on security matters to U.S. agencies from 1955 to 1968, spanning the administrations of Dwight D. Eisenhower, John F. Kennedy, and Lyndon B. Johnson. Appointed by President Richard Nixon as assistant for national security affairs in 1968, Kissinger came to serve as head of the National Security Council (1969-1975), and as secretary of state (September 1973-January 20, 1977). He initially advocated a hardline policy in Vietnam, and helped to engineer the U.S. bombing of Cambodia (1969-70), but he then went on to play a major role in Nixon's "Vietnamization" policy. On January 23, 1973, following several months of negotiations with the North Vietnamese government in Paris, he initiated a ceasefire agreement that provided for the withdrawal of U.S. troops and outlined the machinery for a peace settlement between the two Vietnams. He was awarded a Nobel Peace Prize for this achievement.

LEBANON

SYRIA

Haifa

SEA OF GALILEE

Jordan River

Tel Aviv

Amman

GAZA STRIP

Jerusalem

MEDITERRANEAN SEA

DEAD SEA

Port Said

ISRAEL

NEGEV DESERT

JORDAN

Suez Canal

Mitla Pass

Suez

SAUDI ARABIA

SINAI PENINSULA

Eilat

Aqaba

GULF OF SUEZ

EGYPT

Sharm el Sheikh

RED SEA

Israeli territory in 1948
Arab attacks in 1948
Territory gained by Israel in the war of 1948
Israeli attacks in 1956

0   100 mi
0   60 km

---

establish a foothold on the west bank of the Suez Canal. This cut off the Egyptian Third Army on the east bank of the canal and left the Egyptian capital, Cairo, virtually at Israel's mercy. At the same time, the Israelis fought their way forward into Syria, threatening the Syrian capital, Damascus.

With the United States and the Soviet Union thoroughly committed to the opposing sides in the war, it became urgent to conclude a ceasefire to avoid the risk of a global war. The Arab oil states had also begun to stop shipments of oil to Western Europe and to North America. A ceasefire was eventually agreed by both sides on October 22.

Although Israel had once more ended up as the victor, the Yom Kippur War was a severe blow to Israeli morale. Israeli losses of 1,854 dead were high by their standards. The Arab states, meanwhile, had gained immense prestige by surprising Israel.

CIA COUP IN CHILE

The rise to power of the Marxist Salvador Allende in the 1970 Chilean elections alarmed U.S. president Richard Nixon, who feared that the left-wing regime might form close ties with the Soviet Union. Nixon was determined to overthrow Allende.

On September 10, 1973, Chilean Navy ships conducted joint maneuvers with U.S. warships off the coast. That night, those same Chilean ships returned to the port of Valparaiso. Early on September 11, naval officers seized control of Valparaiso, and by daybreak a swift and bloody coup was underway. Allende rushed to his presidential palace, La Moneda, to take charge of the resistance. La Moneda was then bombed by the Chilean Air Force and the democratically elected president was killed.

THE COUNTRIES
OF SOUTH AMERICA

PINOCHET

General Augusto Pinochet, the Chilean commander-in-chief and a member of the military junta, appointed himself the new president of Chile after the coup of 1973. His first cabinet was made up almost entirely of military officers. Reports claimed that thousands had died, but the military junta said that fewer than 100 people had lost their lives in the CIA-backed uprising. Thousands of Chileans sympathetic to the socialist government were detained. Many were tortured, and several hundred were tried and executed by military war tribunals. Once in power, Pinochet's regime was characterized by brutal repression and 3,000 people were killed or disappeared during his 17 years of rule. He died in 2006.

FALL OF SOUTH VIETNAM

By March 1973, all U.S. ground forces had departed from Vietnam, even though many North Vietnamese Army (NVA) forces remained in South Vietnam. Most of the South Vietnamese commanders realized that, with the withdrawal of the U.S. presence, it was now simply a matter of time before the NVA would begin a major military campaign. Despite the fact that South Vietnamese forces (the ARVN) had held their own during the North's Easter offensive of March–June 1972, only with the aid of U.S. air power could the South hope to push back the NVA. As the events of 1975 indicated, however, the refusal of the United States to intervene doomed South Vietnam. The NVA waited for the signal to strike south in what it initially thought would be a two-year campaign. Much to its surprise, the conquest of South Vietnam took North Vietnamese forces just four months.

A rapid collapse

The seizure of the provincial capital of Phuoc Long on January 6, 1975, signaled the beginning of the end. Located north of the capital city, Saigon, Phuoc Long was considered by the ARVN to be "untenable in case of a heavy attack, due to its geographical position." It was isolated and practically encircled by enemy forces for months before its capture. Vital supplies had to be flown in or sent in by road convoys, which required the provision of armed escorts. Phuoc Long was considered by ARVN commanders to be "weakly defended" and "offered little resistance."

The NVA's seizure of Phuoc Long was designed to test the will of the South's armed forces and also to gauge the reaction of the United States. The loss of Phuoc Long was the first time during the whole of the Vietnam War that an entire province had been lost to the communists. This was obviously a flagrant violation of the ceasefire agreement by the communists, and yet ARVN forces chose not to react militarily while the United States made no significant move to deter the communist advance. In the words of the South Vietnamese president, Nguyen Van Thieu, while it was not "impossible to reoccupy Phuoc Long," from a military standpoint "it was not worthwhile," as to do so would have required troops to be redeployed from other critical areas of defense. NVA forces then began an unstoppable advance. On March 10, the NVA attacked Ban Me Thuot, at the start of its 1975 Spring Offensive. On March 19, the South Vietnamese Army abandoned Quang Tri City and its province. On March 24, Quang Ngai City and Tam Ky fell to the advancing NVA. The next day, Hue City was captured by the NVA. On March 30, the NVA entered Da Nang City and captured the Da Nang Air Base. The ARVN was now collapsing. On the last day of April 1975, the North Vietnamese Army entered Saigon (now named Ho Chi Minh City) and arrested General Minh, the president. The Vietnam War was over.

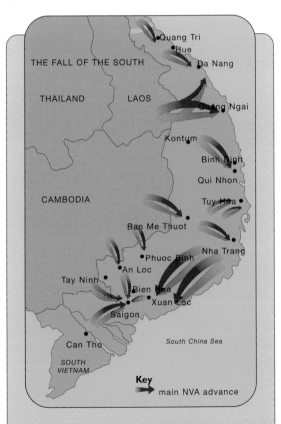

THE FALL OF THE SOUTH

THAILAND

LAOS

CAMBODIA

Quang Tri
Hue
Da Nang
Quang Ngai
Kontum
Binh Dinh
Qui Nhon
Tuy Hoa
Ban Me Thuot
Nha Trang
Phuoc Binh
An Loc
Tay Ninh
Bien Hoa
Xuan Loc
Saigon
Can Tho

SOUTH VIETNAM

South China Sea

Key
→ main NVA advance

THE KHMER ROUGE

The communist Khmer Rouge came to power in Cambodia in 1975, and the brutal regime would go on to claim the lives of more than a million people. Under its Marxist leader, Pol Pot, the Khmer Rouge tried to take Cambodia back to the Middle Ages. Declaring that the nation would start again at "Year Zero," Pol Pot isolated his people from the world and set about emptying the cities, abolishing money, private property, and religion, and setting up rural collectives. Anyone thought to be an intellectual was killed. Often people were condemned for simply wearing glasses or for knowing a foreign language. The Khmer Rouge government was finally overthrown in 1979 by invading Vietnamese troops.

In the 1950s and 1960s, rival guerrilla groups began to fight for independence in the African country of Angola. The first group was the MPLA or Movimento Popular de Libertação de Angola (Popular Liberation Movement of Angola), founded in 1956 and supported by the Soviet Union. In 1957, the FNLA or Frente Nacional de Libertação de Angola (National Front for the Liberation of Angola) was set up with aid from the USA. In 1966, UNITA or União Nacional para a Independencia Total de Angola (National Union for the Total Independence of Angola) was established. UNITA had little foreign aid, but considerable tribal allegiance in southern Angola.

In 1975, Angola became independent after a civil war between these groups. The MPLA, in possession of the capital and with support from the Soviet Union and Cuba, declared itself the government of Angola. Agostinho Neto, a distinguished poet who had led the MPLA since 1962, became president. However, UNITA and the FNLA set up a rival government in the mountainous region of Huambo, where they enlisted the support of South African forces in neighboring Namibia to try to oust the Marxist MPLA.

The conflict in Angola thus became an extension of the Cold War. The United States sent funds to UNITA and the FNLA and encouraged South African involvement. The Soviets provided similar support to the MPLA, while Cuban president Fidel Castro, eager to spread communism in Africa, sent large contingents of Cuban troops to Angola. As early as November 1975, South African and Cuban troops clashed in a battle at Ebo, with victory going decisively to the Cubans.

THE SUPERPOWERS IN AFRICA

In the 1970s, the so-called "Third World" became the new battlefield of the Cold War. After the American debacle in Vietnam and the brutal suppression of Allende's elected Marxist revolution in Chile, by 1973 southern Africa had become the theater for ideological confrontation. Here, the potent cocktail of European decolonisation, postindependent nation-state construction, and the determined resistance of white minority regimes encouraged local guerrilla leaders to look to external sources for patronage and support in their individual struggles. The ability of these local leaders to draw upon global rivals such as the United States, the Soviet Union (and its Eastern bloc allies), Yugoslavia, Cuba, and China for assistance and support proved disastrous for regional peace, but decisive in obliging the white minority regimes to bring blacks into government to counter the pressures from global liberation movements.

NUCLEAR DOCTRINE IN THE 1970s

After the SALT talks in 1970, the United States increased the pace of the nuclear arms race with the deployment of Minuteman III missiles, with multiple independently targetable reentry vehicles (MIRVs). The Anti-Ballistic Missile (ABM) Treaty, designed to halt a nuclear arms race, was also signed. The United States and Soviet Union then signed another treaty, The Prevention of Nuclear War, in June 1973, agreeing to "remove the danger of nuclear war and the use of nuclear weapons."

In 1974, the United States announced a doctrine of "limited strike options," in which a range of deterrents would be available before massive retaliation was considered. Later, the United Nations held its first Special Session on Disarmament. Its statement, issued on June 30, 1978, said that "removing the threat of a world war—a nuclear war—is the most urgent task of the present day." In June 1978, the SALT II Treaty restricted the number of strategic offensive weapons the United States and the Soviet Union could possess. However, each side still had thousands of nuclear warheads.

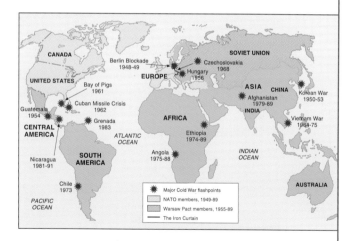

THE IRANIAN REVOLUTION

Female Iranian Muslim fighters in the capital, Tehran, during the revolution that brought Ayatollah Khomeini to power. Overnight Iran went from being a U.S. ally to a staunch enemy.

After dissolving parliament in 1961, the Shah of Iran took control of the country. Opposition was strong, fanned by Shiite Muslims, who were directed from France by the exiled Muslim cleric Ayatollah Ruhollah Khomeini. The Shah's regime, supported by the United States, became increasingly repressive and, in 1978, riots led to virtual civil war. In 1979, the Shah was forced to leave. Khomeini returned in triumph in February 1979 to preside over the establishment of an Islamic republic. On November 4, 1979, after the Shah entered the United States, Iranian students stormed the U.S. Embassy in Tehran, taking 90 Americans hostage. The militants demanded the Shah be turned over to face trial. Some of the hostages were released, but 53 were held. President Jimmy Carter ordered a military rescue that failed, with the death of eight U.S. servicemen.

ABM TREATY

This treaty of "unlimited duration" between the U.S. and the Soviet Union limited each side's anti-ballistic missile (ABM) systems in order to prevent the deployment of nationwide ABM defenses or a base for such a system. Each superpower was restricted to a single deployment area of 100 ABM launchers and missiles. The treaty prohibited the development, testing, and deployment of space-based, sea-based, air-based, and mobile land-based systems and components. Compliance was monitored by national technical means of verification and overseen by a Standing Consultative Commission. The treaty came into force on October 3, 1972.

IRAQ AND THE UNITED STATES

The Iranian Revolution marked a fundamental change in the dynamics of the Persian Gulf region and the attitude of the United States. For Washington, the danger lay not simply in the possible spread of the Islamic Revolution. For its oil supplies, the United States was particularly reliant upon Saudi Arabia, which experienced wide-scale riots in Shiite regions in late 1979 and 1980, threatening the rule of the Saudi monarchy. Bahrain and Kuwait faced similar internal conflicts.

With the Iranian revolution, the interests of the United States and those of Saddam Hussein's government in Iraq became very similar. The Khomeini regime saw Hussein and his government as one of its principal enemies and encouraged the Shiite opposition within Iraq. The United States wanted to contain and reverse a growing threat to its oil supplies.

THE SOVIET INVASION OF AFGHANISTAN

In December 1979, Soviet paratroopers landed in Kabul, the capital of Afghanistan, a country already in the grip of a civil war. The prime minister, Hazifullah Amin, had tried to sweep aside Muslim tradition within the nation and, as a result, many Afghan Muslims joined the Mujahideen, a religiously inspired guerrilla force who wanted the overthrow of the Amin government. The Mujahideen declared a jihad—a holy war—on the supporters of Amin, and this was extended to Soviet forces who were now in Afghanistan trying to maintain the Amin government in power. On December 27, 1979, however, Amin was shot by the Soviets and replaced by Babrak Kamal. His position as head of the Afghan government depended entirely on the fact that he needed 85,000 Soviet soldiers to keep him in power.

The Mujahideen proved to be a formidable opponent. They were equipped with old rifles, but had a knowledge of the mountains around Kabul and the

Russian troops march through an Afghan town following the 1979 Soviet invasion of the country. The Soviets found it impossible to defeat the Afghan resistance, the Mujahideen.

weather conditions that would be encountered there. The Soviets resorted to using napalm, poison gas, and helicopter gunships against the Mujahideen, but they began to experience exactly the same military scenario that the Americans had done in Vietnam.

By 1982, the Mujahideen controlled 75 percent of Afghanistan, despite fighting the might of the world's second most potent military superpower.

THE MUJAHIDEEN

The Mujahideen were a mixture of Afghan resistance fighters, Afghan refugees who had crossed into Pakistan at the onset of the Soviet invasion and later been recruited to fight the Soviets, and Islamists and Muslims from other Arab nations who answered the international call to jihad against the Soviet Union. Contrary to popular myth, most Mujahideen fighters were not Islamic radicals but a group of loosely allied Afghan tribes. The Mujahideen received significant financial and military support from various nations and individuals. The United States supported them primarily through the CIA. This was controversial because the Mujahideen clearly were no more accepting of U.S. culture than they were of Soviet values. However, compared to the risks of the Soviet threat, "the relatively new threat of Islamic fundamentalism" was inconsequential. Defeating communism was the main thrust of U.S. foreign policy, and so the threat of Islamism was ignored. The United States would come to regret this many years later.

In the U.S. presidential election held in 1980, Republican candidate Ronald Reagan capitalized on the U.S. public's fear of Soviet assertiveness and achieved victory over the incumbent, Jimmy Carter. Throughout most of Reagan's administration over the next eight years, it appeared that the pattern of confrontation and détente of the previous two decades was to recur. Instead of simply another rotation in a repeating cycle, however, the 1980s became the final days of the Cold War.

The Reagan administration began by formally declaring détente dead and embarking on the largest peacetime military buildup in U.S. history. In the eight years that followed—from 1981 to 1988—the United States increased its spending on the military from about $117 billion to approximately $290 billion per year. "We do not know how much time we have left," Secretary of Defense Caspar Weinberger regularly warned Congress, as he argued for approval of the additional appropriations.

A new Cold War?

Ronald Reagan employed some of the harshest anti-Soviet rhetoric used by a U.S. official since the early 1960s. He boldly asserted that Soviet leaders "reserve unto themselves the right to commit any crime, to lie, to cheat." He proclaimed in a speech to the British parliament in 1982 that, "The Soviet Union runs against the tide of human history." Reagan's strident anticommunist line alarmed some Americans and Europeans, and during the years 1982 to 1984, some of the largest antiwar demonstrations of the entire Cold War period occurred in cities across Europe and the United States.

Even as he identified in his speech to the British parliament "a great revolutionary crisis" within the Soviet system, Reagan did not predict its imminent collapse. However, the selection of Mikhail Gorbachev as the new General Secretary of the Communist Party

Soviet forces in Afghanistan. In 1989, having lost 15,000 dead, the Russians withdrew from the country. As well as the human cost, the vast financial outlay contributed toward the eventual collapse of the Soviet Union in 1991.

of the Soviet Union in March 1985 set in motion the death of Soviet-style communism and marked the beginning of the end of the Cold War.

On achieving power in the Soviet Union, Mikhail Gorbachev quickly recognized that his nation's economy simply could not bear the burden of a continuing arms race with the much richer and more technologically advanced United States. However, Gorbachev and Reagan moved slowly and uneasily toward détente, initially with summit meetings in 1985 in Geneva and Reykjavik.

Thereafter, the pace of accommodation quickened markedly. The two sides concluded an Intermediate Nuclear Forces Treaty in December 1987, eliminating a whole class of ballistic missiles that were stationed in Europe. As a result, Reagan and Gorbachev both received heroes' welcomes when they visited each other's capital cities.

1989, the deciding year

Americans, Europeans, and Soviets all realized that the Cold War was ending when a series of peaceful revolutions swept Eastern Europe in 1989, eradicating Soviet-style communism from countries such as East Germany, Czechoslovakia, and Bulgaria. However, in Poland, Hungary, and Romania change was less peaceful. In Romania, for example, the ruling dictator and brutal tyrant Nicolae Ceausescu and his wife were quickly tried and then executed on Christmas Day 1989.

Earlier, in November 1989, the great symbol of the Cold War era, the Berlin Wall, came down to the cheering of vast crowds. George Bush Sr., the new U.S. president, adjusted slowly to the Cold War's inevitable end. Bush had formed a close friendship with Mikhail Gorbachev by 1990 and backed the Soviet leader in 1991, even to the point of refraining from verbally supporting democrats within the Soviet Union. However, as the Soviet Union began to dissolve, the United States did help new Russian president Boris Yeltsin to resist a communist coup d'etat in August 1991. Gorbachev resigned on December 25, 1991, and the Soviet Union finally died on December 31. The Cold War was over.

SOLIDARITY IN POLAND

Established in Poland in September 1980 at the Gdansk shipyards, Solidarity was an independent labor union. In July 1980, the Polish government, facing an economic crisis, was again forced to raise the price of goods while curbing wages. This was the last straw for much of Poland's labor force, and strikes spread across the country, despite the absence of any organized network. Led by electrician Lech Walesa, a quarter of the population eventually joined Solidarity, including 80 percent of Poland's workforce.

In response, the Soviets gave power to President General Wojciech Jaruzelski, expecting a crackdown on the Solidarity movement. On December 13, 1981, Jaruzelski declared martial law and arrested 5,000 Solidarity members. This resulted in outrage around the globe, with world leaders and many others all voicing support for Solidarity's cause. U.S. president Ronald Reagan imposed sanctions on Poland, which would eventually force the government to soften its policies.

Martial law was lifted on July 22, 1983, yet many restrictions on civil liberties and political life remained. By 1988, Poland's economy was worse than ever, due to foreign sanctions. On August 26, the government announced it was ready to negotiate with Solidarity. On April 17, 1989, Solidarity was legalized.

Solidarity representative Tadeusz Mazowiecki was elected to power on December 31, 1989, becoming the country's first noncommunist prime minister since 1945, and the first in Eastern Europe for more than 40 years. Under Mazowiecki, a Solidarity-led government was formed, with only Jaruzelski remaining from the old regime. Communism had collapsed in Poland and soon the infamous Berlin Wall would meet the same fate.

1980 OLYMPICS

The 1980 Moscow Olympics are perhaps best remembered for the U.S.-led boycott that saw only 81 out of 147 nations compete, the lowest number since the 1956 event in Melbourne. The boycott was in protest of the Soviet invasion of Afghanistan the year before, one of the many conflicts that took place as the Americans and Soviets battled by proxy during the Cold War years. Allies such as Britain and France also condemned the Afghan invasion, but allowed their athletes to compete nonetheless. In 1984, the Olympics were held in Los Angeles. Perhaps predictably, the Soviet Union boycotted them, citing concerns over the safety of their athletes in what they termed an anticommunist environment. However, it was widely regarded as a retaliatory move for the 1980 U.S. boycott.

CRUISE vs SS-20

American Cruise missiles. Though they are no longer deployed in Western Europe, they are still used by U.S. forces, most notably in Iraq and Afghanistan.

By the mid-1970s, it had become clear to NATO planners that the leadership of the Soviet Union intended to undertake a concerted effort to modernize its Intermediate-range Nuclear Force (INF) targeted on NATO members in Europe. Up until that time, the most threatening weapons that had been aimed at Western Europe were the single-warhead SS-4 and SS-5 theater missiles, based at vulnerable fixed launch sites. In 1977, however, Soviet forces began to field the new SS-20, a missile fitted with three accurate, independently targetable warheads. Worse, its launcher was highly mobile, allowing the missiles to be moved around at times of increased international tension, making them difficult to target by their enemies. This signified an increase in Soviet firepower on a tremendous scale.

By 1979, the Soviet military had fielded SS-20s in significant numbers. In that year, NATO political leaders agreed on a historic "dual track" approach to solving the problem. One track was political: the West would attempt to engage the Soviet Union in serious talks aimed at curbing the INF forces of both sides. The other track was military: NATO would deploy hundreds of GLCMs (Ground-Launched Cruise Missiles) and Pershing II missiles in Europe, unless Moscow agreed to stop and then reduce its SS-20 deployments. For the Western alliance, the concern went far beyond the need to have equivalent forces. NATO's chief worry was that, in the nuclear parlance of the time, the Soviet buildup of weapons would "decouple" the defense of Europe from the U.S. strategic nuclear arsenal. In other words, Moscow might believe that it could threaten Western Europe's high-value targets, such as ports, air bases, and similar, with SS-20 nuclear attack potential and not provoke U.S. retaliation, because they were not directly threatening U.S. strategic weapons or territory.

Countering the Soviet threat

The deployment of NATO INF forces was therefore an attempt to make the West's nuclear deterrent more credible by providing military and political leaders with a range of nuclear options short of all-out retaliatory warfare. Western Europe's leaders, in particular, were eager to show the Soviet Union that the continent was still shielded by the U.S. strategic nuclear umbrella, despite the existence of the SS-20 threat. To this end, NATO planners chose to deploy a pair of weapons to counter the Soviet SS-20, because the GLCM and the Pershing II missile systems had very distinctive, complementary characteristics.

The new Pershing missile system was a follow-on to the existing, shorter-range Pershing IA system. As a ballistic missile, Pershing II could offer a high degree of assurance of penetrating any Soviet defenses. In addition, its speed enabled it to threaten the Soviet Union's movable missile launch systems.

Despite historical U.S. influence in Central America, following Fidel Castro's 1959 revolution in Cuba, the Soviet Union saw the region as an ideal breeding ground for communism. For the next 30 years, Soviet agents aided left-wing guerrilla movements in many nations, including Nicaragua and Guatemala. When El Salvador erupted in civil war in 1979, the left-wing Farabundo Marti National Liberation Front (FMLN) guerrillas grew stronger and U.S. Green Beret teams were sent there in 1981 to assist the El Salvadoran Army to defeat this threat. The El Salvadoran Army, though, had a reputation for brutality, as death squads rounded up suspected guerrillas and executed them.

In 1985, the FMLN realized that it could not hope to continue its war against the El Salvadoran Army in a conventional fashion. Although deadly fighting continued for another six years, the FMLN was unable to mount an offensive strong enough to genuinely threaten the El Salvadoran government.

During the 1980s, U.S. elite troops helped to train members of the El Salvadoran Army (above) to fight the guerrillas of the left-wing FMLN.

MARGARET THATCHER

Margaret Thatcher, prime minister of Britain between 1979 and 1990, played a key part in the Cold War. The Soviets had dubbed her the "Iron Lady"–a tag she relished–for the tough line she took against them in speeches shortly after becoming Conservative Party leader in 1975. During the 1980s, Thatcher offered strong support to the defense policies of the U.S. government led by her staunch ally Ronald Reagan.

However, when Mikhail Gorbachev emerged as a potential leader of the Soviet Union, Thatcher invited him to Britain in December 1984 and pronounced him a man she could do business with. She did not yet soften her criticisms of the Soviet system, making use of new opportunities to broadcast to television audiences in Eastern Europe to put the West's case against communism. The United States benefited from Lady Thatcher's support during the tense 1980s.

THE CONTRAS

The various rebel groups opposing Nicaragua's Marxist FSLN (Frente Sandinista de Liberacion Nacional) Sandinista government following the July 1979 overthrow of the U.S.-backed President Somoza were known as the "Contras." Although the Contra movement included many separate groups with different aims and little ideological unity, the Nicaraguan Democratic Force (FDN) emerged as by far the largest. Numbering around 12,000, based in Honduras and funded by the CIA, the Contras blew up bridges, civilian power plants, and schools, burned fields of crops and attacked hospitals. The Contras were responsible for thousands of civilian deaths. According to the Department of State, U.S. military and nonmilitary aid to the Contras amounted to $300 million between 1982 and 1990. The general election of 1990 resulted in defeat for the FSLN and thus the disbanding of the Contras.

During the 1980s there were several high-profile defections by Soviet spies. In 1980, KGB agent Ilya Dzhirkvelov fled the Soviet Union. Five years later, the KGB's Colonel Oleg Gordievsky defected in London and began working for Western intelligence. He then revealed that many British politicians, trade unionists, and journalists were in the pay of Moscow. Similarly, Stanislav Lunev was a Central Intelligence Office colonel prior to his defection to America in 1988.

The defectors provided valuable information to the West, though the KGB remained powerful, because, in the 1980s, the KGB made greater use of electronic espionage—communications intercepts and satellites—to supplement intelligence gathered by agents.

Soviet spy Aldrich Ames (center) used the money he received from the KGB to fund a lavish lifestyle. He is currently serving a life sentence.

ALDRICH AMES

CIA agent Aldrich Ames sold secrets to the Soviets in the 1980s, causing immense damage to the Americans. Known to the KGB by his codename of "The Bell," his actions are thought to have led to the deaths of at least 10 U.S. agents operating in the Soviet Union. He began providing the KGB with the names of CIA spies in April 1985, seeking money to pay off debts. He received an initial payment of $50,000. Ames admitted to receiving a total of about $2.5 million from the Soviet Union during the nine years he acted as a double agent.

He began to spend the money on a lavish lifestyle, including a new Jaguar car, foreign holidays and a new $540,000 house. He never attempted to hide his spending, although his CIA salary was never higher than $70,000 a year. Due to the inability of the CIA to uncover the leak and the fear that the counterintelligence division may not have been secure, the CIA turned to the FBI to investigate the matter. The FBI soon focused on Ames as one of the prime suspects, putting him under constant surveillance. In February 1994, Ames was scheduled to fly to Moscow as part of his duties for the CIA. The FBI feared that he would defect. This led to the arrest of Ames and his wife on February 21, 1994. In the same year, Ames was jailed for life without parole.

The Strategic Defense Initiative (SDI), popularly known as "Star Wars," was a program first initiated on March 23, 1983, by U.S. president Ronald Reagan. The intent of this program was to develop a sophisticated anti-ballistic missile system in order to prevent missile attacks from other countries, specifically the Soviet Union. At the end of the Strategic Defense Initiative, 30 billion dollars had been invested in the program, but no laser-and-mirror system, as had been proposed, was ever used, on land or in space.

Fear of Soviet retaliation due to violations in the ABM treaty from the first SALT talks was a primary factor in these international pressures, but U.S. legislators and members of Congress also argued that the creation of a large anti-ballistic missile system would raise tensions between the two nations and potentially spark a

U.S. President Ronald Reagan (left) photographed with Soviet leader Mikhail Gorbachev.

catastrophic conflict. Because a preemptive strike capability would be advantageous in a nuclear war, both nations were already on edge and so it was decided in the United States that any project that could jeopardize the balance of power would be discarded.

The space-based weapons and laser aspects of the futuristic system gained it the nickname "Star Wars," named after the popular 1977 science-fiction movie.

RONALD REAGAN

The "Reagan Doctrine" was the term used to characterize U.S. president Ronald Reagan's policy of supporting anticommunist insurgents wherever they might be. In his 1985 State of the Union address, Reagan called on Congress and on the U.S. people to stand up to the Soviet Union, a nation he had previously called the "Evil Empire:" "We must stand by all our democratic allies. And we must not break faith with those who are risking their lives—on every continent, from Afghanistan to Nicaragua—to defy Soviet-supported aggression and secure rights which have been ours from birth."

This reiterated statements made in NSC National Security Decision Directive 75. This 1983 directive stated that a central priority of the U.S. administration in its policy toward the Soviet Union would be "to contain and over time reverse Soviet expansionism," particularly in the developing world. As the directive also went on to note: "The U.S. must rebuild the credibility of its commitment to resist Soviet encroachment on U.S. interests and those of its allies and friends, and to support effectively those Third World states that are willing to resist Soviet pressures or oppose Soviet initiatives hostile to the United States, or are special targets of Soviet policy."

American troops during "Operation Urgent Fury," the U.S. invasion of the island of Grenada which toppled a Marxist regime in America's backyard.

In the early 1980s, the Caribbean island of Grenada was run by a left-wing government led by Maurice Bishop. By 1983, his New Jewel Movement (NJM) had alarmed the U.S. by accepting weapons from Cuba. In October Bishop was executed by a faction of the NJM, creating disorder that threatened the lives of U.S. students on the island. In response, and at the request of other Caribbean nations (who supplied some troops), the U.S. then launched "Operation Urgent Fury," sending in an invasion force that eventually totaled 5,000 troops. They encountered about 1,200 Grenadians, 780 Cubans, 49 Soviets, and troops from other communist nations. Within three days, 599 Americans and 80 foreign nationals were evacuated, and U.S.-led forces succeeded in reestablishing a representative form of government in Grenada. An Interim Advisory Council was established, which governed Grenada until late 1984, when Herbert A. Blaize, the head of the New National Party, was elected prime minister.

ATTACK ON LIBYA

The U.S. air attack on Libya in North Africa in April 1986 marked the first major U.S. military response to modern terrorism. The immediate cause was a terrorist bombing in West Berlin 10 days earlier, an incident to which the U.S. linked Soviet-backed Libyan leader Muammar Qadhafi. The April 1986 attack, known as "Operation El Dorado Canyon," involved more than 100 U.S. aircraft. The principal strike force was in the form of Navy A-6s from the aircraft carriers USS *America* and USS *Coral Sea*, and Air Force F-111s from airbases in Britain. The refusal of the French government to grant authority for a U.S. overflight of their country greatly complicated operational matters, and necessitated the refueling of the aircraft for a much longer flight around the Iberian peninsula. Despite this obstacle, the U.S. force was able to launch its attack on Libyan targets at 02:00 hours local time on April 16. Over the course of 12 minutes, U.S. forces dropped 60 tons (61 tonnes) of munitions and encountered negligible resistance from the Libyans.

PERESTROIKA

By the mid-1980s the Soviet Union was in the grip of a serious economic crisis, with falling industrial and agricultural production. Mikhail Gorbachev, the General Secretary of the Communist Party of the Soviet Union and head of state, attempted to reform the entire Soviet economic and political system. "Perestroika" (restructuring) and "glasnost" (openness) were his watchwords for the renovation of the Soviet Union. Economically, the terms referred to the legalization of cooperatives and other semiprivate business ventures, the demonopolization and liberalization of price controls, and the election of enterprise managers.

This program of liberalization then developed into democratization, and the Cold War was over by the end of the 1980s. A major aspect of perestroika in its initial conception was, however, to inject a new dynamism into the Soviet economy. In that respect, Gorbachev's initiatives failed. Indeed, Gorbachev came to believe that the Soviet economic system, just like the political system, needed not reform, but rather to be dismantled and then rebuilt on different foundations.

Unfortunately for the Soviet Union, these reforms had the effect of aggravating the decay of public services, created large-scale unemployment, polarized the people into a minority who found new wealth and the majority who had to endure new levels of poverty, and generated crippling inflation. In short, the program made the former superpower increasingly dependent on foreign relief. Those who gained from the new "market" economy were preeminently well-placed members of the Soviet Communist Party and criminal gangsters.

MIKHAIL GORBACHEV

Mikhail Gorbachev is largely credited with bringing about the end of the Cold War. Born in 1931, he rose to become the general secretary of the Soviet Communist Party, despite being the youngest member of the Politburo. He then put in motion his reformist policies and by 1989 had brought about the end of the Soviet occupation of Afghanistan and had sanctioned the end of the communist monopoly on political power in Eastern Europe. For his huge contribution to reducing East-West tensions, Gorbachev was awarded the 1990 Nobel Peace Prize. By 1990, however, his reform program had failed to deliver significant improvement in the Soviet economy, and the elimination of political and social controls had released latent ethnic and national tensions in the Baltic states, in the constituent republics of Armenia, Georgia, Ukraine, and Moldova, and elsewhere. In 1991, Gorbachev resigned as Russian president. Since 1992 he has headed a number of international organizations.

INF TREATY

U.S. President Ronald Reagan (right) and Soviet General Secretary Mikhail Gorbachev sign the INF Treaty in December 1987.

The Intermediate-Range Nuclear Forces (INF) Treaty between the U.S. and the Soviet Union eliminated all nuclear-armed ground-launched ballistic and cruise missiles with ranges of between 300–3,400 miles (500 and 5,500 km) and their infrastructure. It was the first nuclear arms control agreement actually to reduce nuclear arms, rather than simply to establish ceilings that could not be exceeded.

The INF Treaty was signed by U.S. President Ronald Reagan and Soviet General Secretary Mikhail Gorbachev in Washington, D.C., on December 8, 1987. On January 15, 1988, Reagan signed National Security Directive 296, which instructed Secretary of Defense Frank Carlucci to establish a new agency—the On-Site Inspection Agency (OISA)—to implement the INF Treaty's on-site inspection and escort responsibilities. Thirty days after the INF Treaty entered into force on June 1, 1988, OSIA began inspections of 130 Soviet INF sites in East Germany, Czechoslovakia, and the Soviet Union, and Soviet inspection teams visited 31 INF sites in Britain, the Netherlands, Belgium, Germany, Italy, and the United States.

In all, 2,692 missiles were to be eliminated. In addition, all associated equipment and operating bases were closed for any further INF missile system activity.

Altogether, the INF Treaty resulted in the eventual elimination of 846 U.S. INF missile systems and 1,846 Soviet INF missile systems.

THE NUCLEAR ARSENAL

Nuclear warheads in the 1980s

	USA	USSR	UK	France	China	Total
1980	23,764	30,062	350	250	280	54,706
1981	23,031	32,049	350	275	330	56,035
1982	22,937	33,952	335	275	360	57,859
1983	23,154	35,804	320	280	380	59,938
1984	23,228	37,431	270	280	415	61,623
1985	23,135	39,197	300	360	425	63,416
1986	23,254	40,723	300	355	425	65,056
1987	23,490	38,859	300	420	415	63,484
1988	23,077	37,333	300	410	430	61,549
1989	22,174	35,805	300	410	435	59,124

Thousands of Germans gather to celebrate the end of communism with the symbolic fall of the Berlin Wall.

East German leader Erich Honecker had once stated: "The Berlin Wall will still exist in 50 and in 100 years, unless the reasons for its existence are eliminated." By the 1980s, however, communism in Eastern Europe was politically and economically bankrupt. In East Germany, wages were low and many lived in poverty. Encouraged by Gorbachev's reforms in the Soviet Union, mass protests in the East German cities of Dresden, Leipzig, and Potsdam demanded a free press and the freedom to travel. On Friday, November 9, 1989, Honecker learned that Soviet troops would not support him and he gave in to the demands. That weekend, the East German government opened its borders, allowing its citizens to visit the West. After 28 years, the Berlin Wall had fallen. In March 1990, free elections were held in East Germany and noncommunists gained power. In July, West Germany's deutschemark became the official currency of East and West Germany. In October, East and West Germany were reunited into a single nation.

COMMUNISM FALLS IN EASTERN EUROPE

The fall of the Berlin Wall was just one of many revolutionary changes that swept through Eastern Europe in 1989. In Hungary, the communist government initiated reforms that led to the sanctioning of a multiparty system and free elections. In Poland, the communists entered into talks with the reinvigorated union "Solidarity." Poland then held its first free elections since before World War II, and in 1989 Solidarity formed the first noncommunist government within the Soviet bloc since 1948.

Czechs and Slovaks took to the streets to demand political reforms in Czechoslovakia. Leading the demonstrations in Prague was dissident playwright Vaclav Havel, co-founder of the reform group "Charter 77." The Communist Party of Czechoslovakia peacefully transferred rule to Havel and the Czechoslovak reformers in what was later dubbed the "Velvet Revolution." In Romania, the communist regime of hardliner Nicolae Ceausescu was violently overthrown by the people in December 1989. Soon, the communist parties of Bulgaria and Albania also ceded power. Communism in Eastern Europe had collapsed.

COLLAPSE OF THE SOVIET UNION

Tanks roll into Moscow in August 1991 during the short-lived coup by communist hardliners against Gorbachev's reforms.

When Poles, Czechs, and Hungarians successfully claimed independent statehood in 1989, this had a destabilizing effect within the Soviet Union itself. Lithuanians, Estonians, and Latvians in particular also wanted their independence. In 1990, Boris Yeltsin, chairman of the Russian Supreme Soviet, demanded Russian "sovereignty" from the Soviet Union. In June 1991, Yeltsin was elected president of Russia and demanded full independence.

For hardliners in the KGB (the Soviet secret police) and the Soviet armed forces this was too much and they mounted a coup in August 1991. It began on the 18th, when Mikhail Gorbachev was placed under house arrest in his holiday home on the Crimean coast. However, the dissidents showed a lack of resolution when faced by defiance from Yeltsin and the thousands of Russian citizens who surrounded the parliament

THE COST OF THE COLD WAR

The Cold War was hugely expensive. Estimates indicate that some $8 trillion ($8,000,000,000,000) was spent worldwide on nuclear and other weapons between 1945 and 1996. Although a nuclear catastrophe was averted by the balance of terror, the Cold War's shooting wars did take their toll in the deaths of millions in Korea, in Vietnam, and in Afghanistan; in hundreds of thousands in Angola; in tens of thousands in Nicaragua, El Salvador, and Ethiopia; and in thousands in Hungary and Romania. Civilians accounted for more deaths than soldiers. For decades, the people of Eastern Europe had lived under communism. When they had the chance, they chose democracy. With the dissolution of the Soviet Union in 1991, the United States had seemingly won the Cold War, yet the cost was such that it damaged the U.S. economy long term. China and Japan later emerged to pose an economic threat to the United States in a way that the Soviet Union never did.

building in Moscow, from where Yeltsin was able to speak to the outside world.

The coup had failed by August 22, and within days its leaders were arrested. Yeltsin, with the leaders of the two other Slavic republics, Belarus and Ukraine, then dissolved the Soviet Union. On December 25, 1991, the red flag was lowered from the Kremlin for the last time. By the end of the month, the Soviet Union had passed into history, to be replaced by 15 new countries in a Commonwealth of Independent States.

FURTHER RESOURCES

PUBLICATIONS

Ambrose, Stephen E., Carr, Caleb, Fleming Thomas, and Hanson, Victor, *The Cold War: A Military History*, Random House, London, 2006.

Doherty, Thomas, *Cold War, Cool Medium: Television, McCarthyism, and American Culture*, Columbia University Press, New York, 2005.

Crowley, David, *Posters of the Cold War*, Victoria & Albert Museum, London, 2008.

Field, Douglas, *American Cold War Culture*, Edinburgh University Press, Edinburgh, UK, 2005.

Frankel, Max, *High Noon in the Cold War: Kennedy, Krushchev, and the Cuban Missile Crisis*, Presidio Press, New York, 2005.

Gaddis, John Lewis, *The Cold War: A New History*, Penguin, New York, 2006.

Hanhimaki, Jussi M., and Westad, Odd Arne, *The Cold War: A History in Documents and Eyewitness Accounts*, Oxford University Press, New York, 2004.

Hogan, Michael J., *The End of the Cold War: Its Meaning and Implications*, Cambridge University Press, Cambridge, UK, 1992.

Issacs, Jeremy, and Downing, Taylor, *Cold War: An Illustrated History, 1945-1991*, Little Brown and Company, London, 1998.

Jian, Chen, *Mao's China and the Cold War*, The University of North Carolina Press, Chapel Hill, NC, 2000.

Judt, Tony, *Postwar: A History of Europe Since 1945*, Penguin, New York, 2006.

LaFeber, Walter, *America, Russia and the Cold War 1945-2006*, McGraw-Hill, Maidenhead, UK, 2006.

Levering, Ralph B., *The Cold War: A Post-Cold War History*, Harlan Davidson, Wheeling, Ill, 2005.

McMahon, Robert J., *The Cold War: A Very Short Introduction*, Oxford University Press, New York, 2003.

Matlock, Jack, *Reagan and Gorbachev: How the Cold War Ended*, Random House Trade Paperbacks, London, 2005.

May, Elaine Tyler, *Homeward Bound: American Families in the Cold War Era*, Basic Books, New York, 2008.

Oberdorfer, Don, *From the Cold War to a New Era: The United States and the Soviet Union, 1983-1991*, The Johns Hopkins University Press, Baltimore, Maryland, 1998.

Painter, David, *The Cold War: An International History*, Routledge, New York, 1999.

Powaski, Ronald E., *The Cold War: The United States and the Soviet Union, 1917-1991*, Oxford University Press, New York, 1997.

Sewell, Mike, *The Cold War*, Cambridge University Press, Cambridge, UK, 2001.

Sis, Peter, *The Wall: Growing Up Behind the Iron Curtain*, Farrar, Straus and Giroux, New York, 2007.

Smyser, W.R., *From Yalta to Berlin: The Cold War Struggle Over Germany*, St. Martin's Press, New York, 2000.

Taylor, David, *The Cold War*, Heinemann, Oxford, UK, 2001.

Walker, Martin, *The Cold War: A History*, Holt Paperbacks, New York, 1995.

Westad, Odd Arne, *The Global Cold War: Third World Interventions and the Making of Our Times*, Cambridge University Press, Cambridge, UK, 2007.

Whitfield, Stephen J., *The Culture of the Cold War (The American Moment)*, The Johns Hopkins University Press, Baltimore, Maryland, 1996.

Zubok, Vladislav M., *A Failed Empire: The Soviet Union in the Cold War from Stalin to Gorbachev*, The University of North Carolina Press, Chapel Hill, NC, 2009.

WEBSITES

www.coldwar.org
The Cold War Museum, an organization dedicated to education, preservation, and research on the Cold War.

www.bbc.co.uk/history/worldwars/coldwar
A BBC guide to the key events of the Cold War.

www.ibiblio.org/expo/soviet.exhibit/coldwar.html
Key documents of the Cold War.

www.mtholyoke.edu/acad/intrel/coldwar.htm
Full text original documents relating to the Cold War period. Covers the years from 1945 to 1986.

http://gpweb.us/VLColdWarIndex.htm
History of the Cold War, 1945-1991.

http://history.sandiego.edu/gen/20th/coldwar0.html
Outline of United States and Soviet relations during the Cold War 1945-1991. Includes various photographs and related links.

www.nationalcoldwarexhibition.org.uk
The National Cold War Exhibtion. Includes weapons and timeline.

INDEX

CC